CHRISTIANITY'S AMERICAN FATE

T0003242

ALSO BY DAVID A. HOLLINGER

When This Mask of Flesh Is Broken (2019)

Protestants Abroad (2017)

After Cloven Tongues of Fire (2013)

Cosmopolitanism and Solidarity (2006)

Postethnic America (1995, 2000, and 2006)

Science, Jews, and Secular Culture (1996)

In the American Province (1985)

Morris R. Cohen and the Scientific Ideal (1975)

The American Intellectual Tradition (co-edited with Charles Capper,
    7th ed., 2017)

The Humanities and the Dynamics of Inclusion since World War II
    (edited for the American Academy of Arts and Sciences, 2006)

Reappraising Oppenheimer: Centennial Studies and Reflections
    (co-edited with Cathryn Carson, 2005)

History at Berkeley (with Gene A. Brucker and Henry F. May, 1998)

Christianity's American Fate

HOW RELIGION BECAME MORE CONSERVATIVE AND SOCIETY MORE SECULAR

DAVID A. HOLLINGER

PRINCETON UNIVERSITY PRESS

PRINCETON & OXFORD

Copyright © 2022 by David A. Hollinger

Princeton University Press is committed to the protection of copyright and the intellectual property our authors entrust to us. Copyright promotes the progress and integrity of knowledge. Thank you for supporting free speech and the global exchange of ideas by purchasing an authorized edition of this book. If you wish to reproduce or distribute any part of it in any form, please obtain permission.

Requests for permission to reproduce material from this work should be sent to permissions@press.princeton.edu

Published by Princeton University Press
41 William Street, Princeton, New Jersey 08540
99 Banbury Road, Oxford OX2 6JX

press.princeton.edu

All Rights Reserved

First paperback printing, 2024
Paperback ISBN 978-0-691-23392-5
Cloth ISBN 978-0-691-23388-8
ISBN (e-book) 978-0-691-23389-5

British Library Cataloging-in-Publication Data is available

Editorial: Fred Appel and James Collier
Production Editorial: Jill Harris
Jacket/Cover Design: Heather Hansen
Production: Erin Suydam
Publicity: Maria Whelan and Kathryn Stevens
Copyeditor: Joseph Dahm

Excerpt from "Directive" by Robert Frost from *The Poetry of Robert Frost*, edited by Edward Connery Lathem. Copyright © 1947, 1969 by Henry Holt and Company. Copyright © 1975 by Lesley Frost Ballantine. Reprinted by permission of Henry Holt and Company and Penguin Random House. All Rights Reserved.

This book has been composed in Arno

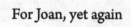
For Joan, yet again

We take captive every thought to make it obedient to Christ.

—2 CORINTHIANS 10:5

Have the courage to use your own understanding.

—IMMANUEL KANT

CONTENTS

PREFACE

WHEN NON-CHRISTIANS learn of disputes between different groups of Christians, they may remark, "I don't have a dog in that fight." But they do. Even in our time, when a smaller percentage of the population than ever before professes the Christian faith, the destiny of the United States as a whole remains significantly determined by individuals and groups who claim the authority to speak for Christianity. Americans in the early twenty-first century find themselves in an increasingly secular society saddled with an increasingly religious politics.

Christianity has become an instrument for the most politically, culturally, and theologically reactionary Americans. White evangelical Protestants were an indispensable foundation for Donald Trump's presidency and have become the core of the Republican Party's electoral strength. They are the most conspicuous advocates of "Christian nationalism." Other kinds of Christians, including Catholics, African American Protestants, and nonevangelical white Protestants, remain active in public life, too. But most of Christianity's symbolic capital has been seized by a segment of the population committed to ideas about the Bible, the family, and civics that most other Americans reject.

How did this happen? *How did Christianity, a vast and multitudinous force in the United States since its beginning, achieve this shape and come to play the role it now does?* This book tries to answer this question, which is much broader than "why did evangelicals flock to Trump?" At issue is not only Christianity's role in contemporary politics, but the historic momentum of the version of this faith that enabled Trump and is almost certain to survive the present moment.

My inquiry is driven by the deepening of what Barack Obama calls the "epistemological crisis" threatening democracy. Millions of Americans believe patent falsehoods and live in epistemic enclosures that keep them from hearing even the most well-substantiated and carefully explained truths about vaccines, climate change, election outcomes, immigration, and a host of other matters of great public concern. What has caused this crisis? Media deregulation, internet anarchy, economic conditions, and racial prejudice are blamed, and rightly so. The culture of evangelical Protestantism is another enabler, often acknowledged, but its role in weakening the critical capacities of many Americans is greater than is usually recognized. Contrary to the view that evangelicalism is a benign presence in American life, hijacked by outsiders, I argue that evangelicalism's history prepared it to be just what it showed itself to be in the era of Donald Trump. *White evangelical Protestantism is not simply white; it is also evangelical.* It took form in a dialectical struggle with a nonevangelical Protestantism led by Americans who were just as white as Billy Graham.

I have told parts of this story before, especially in *After Cloven Tongues of Fire: Protestant Liberalism in Modern American History* (2013) and *Protestants Abroad: How Missionaries Tried to Change the World but Changed America* (2017). But here, in *Christianity's American Fate: How Religion Became More Conservative and Society More Secular*, I offer a more extensive analytic narrative.

My interest in religion and politics goes back to my high school years in Southern California, when I argued with fundamentalist classmates. It was then that I first became aware of the character and significance of what this book calls "the ecumenical-evangelical divide." In informal debates with Southern Baptist youths, I voiced what I understood of liberal theology, and I defended the progressive initiatives endorsed by the *Christian Century*. My fundamentalist friends constantly invoked Billy Graham, but to my dismay none of them had ever heard of the missionary doctor Albert Schweitzer, the great hero of my parents and their circle of churchgoers. At our class's graduation, one Arkansas-born classmate, climaxing four years of more or less genial argumentation, bid me farewell by confidently informing me that people like me "will be destroyed at the battle of Armageddon."

I later drifted away from the faith, but retained a feel for it that I hope informs this book. Although I now write from a secular perspective, I know that I, as a post-Protestant, bring to the historian's vocation a sensibility that owes much to my Protestant background. I have written about the lives of my church-centered family in *When This Mask of Flesh Is Broken: The Story of an American Protestant Family* (2019).

Many colleagues and friends offered suggestions on specific chapters and earlier drafts of this book. I am indebted to Randall Balmer, Dorothy Bass, Margaret Bendroth, Jon Butler, Paul Capetz, Mark Chaves, Elesha Coffman, Joseph Creech, Kristin Kobes Du Mez, Richard Fox, Timothy Gloege, Thomas Albert Howard, James Hudnut-Beumler, Daniel Immerwahr, Slavica Jakelic, James Kloppenberg, Bruce Kuklick, Melani McAlister, Christopher Ocker, Mel Piehl, Robert Post, Richard Rosengarten, Mark Schwehn, Brent Sockness, Werner Sollors, Matthew Sutton, Peter Thuesen, Hannah Waits, Molly Worthen, and Gene Zubovich. The experience of writing this book has been enriched by discussions of its leading ideas with a group of treasured colleagues on my own Berkeley campus: Mark Brilliant, Carol Clover, John Connelly, Brian DeLay, Martin Jay, Thomas Laqueur, Marilyn McEntyre, Daniel Sargent, Ethan Shagan, and Jonathan Sheehan. For excellent advice on many issues, I am indebted to Wendy Strothman of the Strothman Agency, and to Fred Appel of the Princeton University Press. My greatest debt is once again to Joan Heifetz Hollinger, to whom this book is dedicated.

Berkeley, California
March 2022

CHRISTIANITY'S AMERICAN FATE

1

Introduction

THE OTHER PROTESTANTS

"For I was an hungred, and ye gave me meat: I was thirsty, and ye gave me drink: I was a stranger, and ye took me in: Naked, and ye clothed me: I was sick, and ye visited me: I was in prison, and ye came unto me." . . . "Lord, when saw we thee an hungred, and fed thee? or thirsty, and gave thee drink? When saw we thee a stranger, and took thee in? or naked, and clothed thee? Or when saw we thee sick, or in prison, and came unto thee?" . . . "Verily I say unto you, Inasmuch as ye have done it unto one of the least of these my brethren, ye have done it unto me."

—MATTHEW 25:35–40

DONALD TRUMP had good reason, on June 1, 2020, to stand in front of a church on Lafayette Square in Washington, D.C., holding a Bible aloft while cameras recorded the moment. As police and government troops forcibly cleared peaceful civil rights protestors from the square, Trump was proclaiming his connection to the white evangelical voters he knew would appreciate this gesture. Millions of others dismissed Trump's photo op as a cynical caper, but he understood his dependence on a segment of the electorate who stood for a Christian America and believed the Bible belonged to them. Enamored of Trump, few knew that the church was St. John's Episcopal, a bastion of the "other Protestants," the liberal, ecumenical Protestants known for their more inclusive vision of the gospel and of the nation.

What counts as "Christian" is always achieved, never given. It all depends on who gets control of the local franchise. From ancient times to the present, Christianity has been a movement of sensibilities, impulses, ideals, perceptions, loves, hatreds, and programs that are brought into it and are processed by distinctive groups who manage to build a critical mass of people willing to recognize them as Christian. Even Christianity's original, movement-defining documents are themselves of disparate ancestries in the ancient Mediterranean world.[1] The purposes credibly advanced in the name of Jesus of Nazareth are not infinite, but they are staggering in their diversity and range.

In today's United States, Christianity's loudest voices are those of the people to whose sensibilities Trump played that June evening. How did these people gain such power? How did they make so much of the world regard them as synonymous with Christianity writ large? This question demands an inquiry more wide ranging than trying, as many writers have already done very well, to discover Trump's appeal to white evangelicals.[2] Trump took advantage of a white evangelical culture that was well in place before he came along and is likely to remain a factor in American public life after he is gone. That culture's potential durability makes public understanding of its place in the history of American Christianity imperative.

Some aspects of the larger story are widely understood. This was a heavily Protestant country from the start. A

mid-twentieth-century alliance of politically conservative bil-
lionaires and media-savvy preacher-entrepreneurs enabled the
rise of the religious right. Evangelicalism's simplicity and voice
of confident authority offered solace and hope to vulnerable
people vexed by life's genuine mysteries and too often neglected
by the rich and powerful. For some white people, religion was
simply a mask for racism.

All true. But there is more to it.

Evangelicalism achieved its character by rejecting a Christian
alternative with markedly different implications for democracy
and for the boundaries of the national community. Too often
evangelicalism's rise to popularity and influence is narrated in
relative isolation, not in its dialectical relationship with another
Protestantism whose adherents had more respect for modern
science and were more willing to accept ethnoracial diversity.

These other Protestants are commonly called *mainline*, but
ecumenical is a more accurate label. Starting about 1960, *mainline* became a popular term for the denominations understood
to be an informal "Protestant establishment" of long standing.[3]
This meant Methodists, Congregationalists, Presbyterians,
Episcopalians, Northern Baptists, Disciples of Christ, several
Lutheran bodies, and a handful of smaller Calvinist and Ana-
baptist confessions. Yet the label was already anachronistic by
the 1970s, when these groups were losing members and cultural
standing at a rapid rate. These denominations often took liberal
political positions, but *liberal* fails to express a religious quality
that is essential to their distinctive character: a willingness to
cooperate in ecclesiastical, civic, and global affairs with a great
variety of groups that professed to be Christian, and many that
did not. By working with ecumenical organizations like the
Federal and National Councils of Churches, Church World Service, the World Council of Churches, and the United Nations,

and by recognizing the integrity of non-Christian religions, these denominations generated intense opposition from the more sectarian Protestants who in the 1940s insisted on calling themselves *evangelical*, a label that in earlier times was routinely applied to any proselytizing group of Christians. All labels are imperfect and inevitably mask internal differences, but *ecumenical* and *evangelical* are the least confusing terms to denote the two major Protestant groups in the United States, especially since World War II.[4]

Ecumenical Protestantism channeled through Christianity the Enlightenment's critical perspective on belief and its generous view of human capabilities. In so doing, ecumenical Protestantism developed a set of relatively cosmopolitan initiatives that had two decisive consequences for American Christianity and its relation to public life. First, ecumenical ideas largely defined the terms on which evangelicalism took shape and presented itself to American society. Evangelicalism, like its parent, fundamentalism, achieved definition and gained standing as a point-by-point response to the modernizing initiatives of ecumenicals. Second, these efforts to create a more inclusive community of faith and a more pluralistic nation facilitated an out-migration by many "mainliners," who left the churches as they found homes elsewhere, in the cultural domains that ecumenical leaders had engaged sympathetically. Ecumenical preachers and teachers risked their own authority and that of Christianity by accommodating a scientifically advanced and demographically diverse modernity that their evangelical rivals kept at a greater distance. By the end of the twentieth century, the United States had a substantial population of post-Protestants—people significantly shaped by their religious ancestry but no longer affirming the faith.

Did ecumenical Protestants win the country while losing the church?[5] Not quite. But this hyperbole contains an element of truth. By the turn of the twenty-first century the pluralistic, proudly multicultural public life of the United States looked more like what ecumenical leaders of the 1960s wanted than what their contemporary evangelical counterparts advocated. But the evangelicals won in the narrower competition for the loyalties of the minority of Americans who now identify with the Republican Party. Evangelicalism created a safe harbor for white people who wanted to be counted as Christians without having to accept what ecumenical leaders said were the social obligations demanded by the gospel, especially the imperative to extend civil equality to nonwhites. A popular theory of modern religious history holds that evangelical churches flourished because they made greater demands on the faithful, while liberal churches declined on account of not demanding much of anything.[6] The opposite is true. Evangelicalism made it easy to avoid the challenges of an ethnoracially diverse society and a scientifically informed culture. Moreover, it is a mistake to suppose that evangelicalism has been hijacked by outsiders. Evangelical numbers swelled during the era of Donald Trump, but those who adopted evangelical identity anew had good reason to do so. What they were joining was easily recognized.[7] These clear alignments gave credibility to historian Jon Meacham's observation that in the election of 2020, "the Enlightenment is on the ballot."[8]

Understanding the American fate of Christianity also requires careful attention to Christianity's own shifting demographics. Race does not explain everything, but it is entwined with religion at virtually every point in the history of the United States. Ethnoreligious groups carrying their own priorities and sensibilities exercised different measures of influence over Christianity at different times. The white Protestants who ran the country well into the twentieth century were predominantly the biological

and cultural descendants of the "dissenters" from the established churches of England and Continental Europe. These
Calvinists, Anabaptists, and Wesleyans built a white Protestant
tent big enough to nurture both liberal-ecumenical and
conservative-evangelical persuasions. Eventually, two other
major demographic groups diversified American Christianity.
African American Protestants, long denied civil rights, economic opportunities, and education, became major participants in the community of faith. Catholics—white, Black, and
Brown—emerged from relative marginality to do the same.

In addition, two non-Christian groups came to influence
how these several kinds of Christians understood themselves
and their shared nation. Jewish immigrants and their descendants achieved prominence in many arenas of public life. Simultaneously, American missionaries abroad made US Christians
aware of Asian peoples who practiced non-Christian faiths.
Many of the missionaries (and even more of their sons and
daughters) came to argue that American interests were more in
line with decolonizing non-Christian nonwhites than with the
old European imperial powers that remained the chief US allies
during the Cold War. These two encounters with non-
Christians—Jews close-up and adherents of other religions at
long distance—had an especially strong effect on the most
highly educated ecumenical Protestants. They developed antiracist programs and criticized the idea of a "Christian America"
because it could not be expected to treat Jews and other non-
Christians as equal citizens. In frequent alliance with liberal
Catholics, secular and religious Jews, and the Black Civil Rights
Movement, the ecumenical Protestant leadership espoused positions on race, gender, sexuality, empire, economics, and divinity
that generated adamant opposition from white evangelicals.

The edifice of American Christianity was hollowed out by the departure of the post-Protestants and of the smaller number of cradle Catholics who left their natal churches. The space vacated in this commodious religious edifice was easily occupied by white evangelicals allied with conservative Catholics on issues of sexuality, gender, and the limits of civic authority. This evangelical takeover of Christian real estate was financed by corporate interests eager to exploit "religious liberty" as an instrument for overturning the regulatory regime of the New Deal. The Republican Party's connection to evangelicals predated Trump and was enabled by the suspicions of federal power common to white citizens of the evangelically intensive southern states. Trump tightened the connection between evangelicalism and economic conservatism, but the connection was ready-made for him.

While the Republican Party became more Christian in its self-representation, the Democratic Party, reflecting the secularization and diversification of American society, offered a political home not only for the rapidly growing ranks of post-Protestants and post-Catholics but also for remnants of the once-formidable white ecumenical Protestant community as well as for liberal Catholics, secular and religious Jews, and the great majority of African Americans who, while often conservative theologically, were strikingly independent of white evangelicals.

Christianity's destiny has been determined by a number of forces, but this book does not treat Christianity as entirely epiphenomenal. A reluctance to take religion seriously inhibits searching inquiries into the political role of Christianity. In this too-common methodological outlook, any religion is unworthy of rigorous scrutiny. Economics, race, social structure, and the like explain history; religion is never a constellation of elements that demand analysis. But secular avoidance is too often answered with religious apologetics. Scholarship in the apologetic tradition focuses on the details of what American Christians have done and makes little effort to identify or explain the role those actions have played in a national or global narrative except to celebrate them and to wish they had been even more influential than they have been. The result is an exceptionally distended public understanding of how Christianity has sustained itself—and in just what configurations—in America's late twentieth- and early twenty-first-century national life.

White evangelical Protestantism is not the only cause of what Barack Obama calls the nation's "epistemological crisis" threatening American democracy.[9] Secularists on the political left are not immune to the temptation for an epistemic closure inimical to civic health. Some of them assert too sweepingly that science and scholarship mask patriarchy, colonialism, and white supremacy.[10] But by any measure, evangelical Protestant leaders have done much more than overzealous progressives to create and shape today's crisis of democracy. The white evangelicals who have controlled the Christian franchise in the United States in recent decades have provided decisive support to a Republican Party committed, for overwhelmingly nonreligious reasons, to the rule of a minority empowered by the anachronisms of the Electoral College. Prominent evangelicals, moreover, have seen fit to aid the Republican cause by participating in the dissemination of misinformation of all sorts—from unfounded accusations of election fraud to lies about COVID vaccines—thereby diminishing the capacity of millions of the faithful to distinguish truth from falsehood.

Some evangelical leaders have reacted with holy horror. They have lamented, in the words of historian Mark Noll, the "intellectual self-immolation" of evangelicalism.[11] Geneticist Francis

Collins, an evangelical who served under both President Trump and President Biden as director of the National Institutes of Health, has consistently condemned the antiscientific, antidemocratic activities of his fellow evangelicals and asked that they take to heart a scripture that is a special favorite of ecumenicals, John 8:32: "Ye shall know the truth and the truth shall make you free."[12]

Noll and Collins remind us that not all evangelicals had sympathy for the riot of January 6, 2021, incited by President Donald Trump in support of his false claim that he had won the 2020 election. But a great many evangelicals believed his lie, and some applauded the riot. Many who stormed the Capitol prominently displayed Christian imagery. The QAnon conspiracy fantasies of the Trump era had many sources outside Christianity, but these fantasies found great traction among people whose spiritual diet had been dominated by evangelical preachers who were bound only loosely by modern standards of plausibility.[13] Exactly what those standards are will always be a matter of some contention. Yet when pollsters report that millions of Americans believe patent falsehoods that affect the interests of the entire society, we do not need to resolve the epistemological disputes between Hume and Hegel in order to appreciate the value of education for the survival of democracy. Education affects the answer to historian Jill Lepore's question: will this country "be governed by reflection and election, by reason and truth, rather than by accident and violence, by prejudice and deceit"?[14]

"The credulous man," wrote W. K. Clifford, "is father to the liar and cheat."[15]

2

A Country Protestant on Steroids

No one will be able to stand against you all the days of your
life. As I was with Moses, so I will be with you; I will never
leave you nor forsake you.

—JOSHUA 1:5

A COMBINATION of three conditions made the United States
from its early years unique in the historically Christian world:
(1) a religiously engaged culture of "dissent," (2) church-state
separation, and (3) massive immigration. No other nation or
empire, including Canada, which came the closest, experienced
this particular combination with equal intensity.

The society of British North America and the nation created
out of its thirteen colonies was dominated by Protestant "dissenters," named for the religious communities they built outside
the established churches of England and Continental Europe.
The Congregationalists, Presbyterians, Baptists, Methodists,
and Quakers dissented from the Church of England. In the
New World, members of these groups lived alongside Mennonites, Moravians, Huguenots, and others who had dissented
from Lutheran and Catholic establishments on the Continent.

Dissenting Protestantism entailed a more intense religiosity than was the norm among nondissenting Protestants. The latter did not strive, as dissenters did, to distinguish themselves from some empowered religious regime. This heightened religious consciousness was then reinforced by the act of leaving an ancestral domain to help populate a new land that was defined in part by its greater opportunities for religious particularism. In a settler society that pushed aside or killed the Indigenous population, these dissenting Protestants easily achieved a measure of control over public life that endured well into the twentieth century. They took the land and on it built a country largely in their own image.

Some of these dissenting Protestants would have been happy with an established church, if it could be their own. But when the United States was founded in a society with so many different confessions, any ecclesiastical establishment was out of the question. The First Amendment to the US Constitution was prompted in part by the secular leanings of some of the founders, but the devout realized that it was a practical necessity: "Congress shall make no law respecting an established religion, or prohibiting the free exercise thereof." This restraint on the national government did not prevent state governments from using tax money to support particular churches, as several states did until 1833, when the last of these, Massachusetts, ceased to support the Congregationalists. Even with the end of established churches at the level of individual states, however, a generalized Protestantism saturated public life. What historian David Sehat calls a "moral establishment" was firmly in place in every state, compromising church-state separation to a degree not recognized until well into the twentieth century.[1]

Yet, by formally separating the federal government from religion, the First Amendment left churches free to perform a function they were less able to perform in countries where religion was part of the state. Churches in the United States could serve as intermediate solidarities, mediating between the kinship network and the nation.

Immigration made this mediation more important than it otherwise would have been. The United States received wave after wave of people who left behind, in their societies of origin, the structures for intimacy and belonging on which they had previously depended. Immigrants were obliged to build replacement structures for themselves. Independent churches were ideal for this purpose. Immigrant groups organized churches by ethnicity, providing individuals with opportunities to be deeply part of something larger than their extended families yet smaller and much more intimate than the country as a whole. These churches were the voluntary associations that, in Tocqueville's view, made the United States unique in world history.[2]

Lutherans, while emerging from a European experience of establishment, became de facto dissenters, accountable to no state church and dividing themselves up according to ethnicity—a Swedish Lutheran synod, a Danish Lutheran synod, a German Lutheran synod, and so forth. Thus in America Lutherans became independent communities, like the Congregationalists and the Baptists. The Episcopalians inherited the traditions of the established Church of England, but they too adjusted to the pluralism of American Protestantism.

Catholic immigrants and their descendants also looked to their churches as intermediate solidarities in Tocqueville's sense, often organized on an ethnic basis, as Polish, Italian, or Irish parishes. These parish-centered communities were all the more vital given the frequent hostility Catholics experienced at the hands of the majority Protestants. New confessions formed, too, creating communities based on experiences in the New World. These included churches formed by the descendants of captured and enslaved Africans, including the African Methodist Episcopal Church, the largest of the predominantly Black denominations. By 1906, the AME counted nearly half a million members, had created Wilberforce University in Ohio, and was cooperating with Black Protestants abroad. Other new denominations included the Mormons, the Seventh-day Adventists, and the Disciples of Christ. Denominationalism flourished in the United States as nowhere else.

The need for intimacy and belonging led to many schisms, as smaller collectives formed to reflect their own perceived priorities, rendering the nation an ever denser expanse of religiously defined communities. By the time of the Civil War, the largest Baptist, Methodist, and Presbyterian bodies had divided themselves not only into northern and southern denominations in relation to the conflict over slavery, but into numerous smaller confessions defined by often minute differences in ritual practice and doctrine. The federal census of 1890 found seventeen Methodist bodies (four of which were African American), thirteen Baptist bodies (one African American), and twelve Presbyterian bodies. Even the less numerous Mennonites divided themselves into a dozen groups wanting to be identified as distinctive denominations.[3]

At the start of the twentieth century the United States was a much more churchgoing, Christianity-affirming country than it had been at the end of the eighteenth.[4] Church-state separation, immigration, and a culture of dissent had created a country Protestant on steroids. It is no wonder that Max Weber, visiting the United States in 1904, was struck by how extensively the lives of Americans were affected by membership in voluntary religious groups.[5] Like Tocqueville seven decades before, the great German scholar understood that religion made America different.

The religious imagery of the Civil War illustrates how the United States gradually became more intensely Christian than it had been at the time of the nation's birth. The founding generation invoked the deity as a matter of routine, but by the 1860s the Bible was a more substantial part of American culture, North and South. Lincoln took for granted something he flagged explicitly in his Second Inaugural Address: that both sides "read the same Bible" and prayed "to the same God." Only in an America much changed from the 1780s could partisans of the Union welcome Julia Ward Howe's incandescently Christian "Battle Hymn of the Republic": "He is trampling out the vintage where the grapes of wrath are stored . . . I have read a fiery gospel writ in burnished rows of steel." As Christ "died to make men holy, let us die to make men free."

A peculiarity in the structure of authority in most American denominations protected Christianity from some of the critical scrutiny it received from the intelligentsias of Western Europe. Governance arrangements in churches in the dissenting tradition were relatively democratic, giving the people in pews more power than was the case not only in the Roman Catholic Church but in the top-down polities of the Lutherans and Anglicans. The dissenting churches conferred large measures of juridical authority on local congregations and on regional parachurch associations. This was especially notable in the many Baptist bodies, as well as among the uniquely influential Congregationalists of New England and to only a slightly lesser extent among the Presbyterians. Preachers and professors had to pay attention to the dispositions of rank-and-file church members and regional associations. The clergy could not get too far out in front of their constituencies without endangering their standing as leaders and their livelihoods as salaried employees.

Preachers had to be especially cautious about two major intellectual developments of the nineteenth century that potentially threatened the faith of churchgoers. One was the Darwinian revolution in natural history. Many clergymen denounced evolution altogether. Others assured the faithful that Genesis need not be taken literally, that evolution was consistent with God's supervision of a steadily improving world, and that Darwin's harsh mechanism of natural selection was only part of the picture. But until the rapid expansion of high school education early in the twentieth century, much of the public paid little attention to evolution. Preachers were able to keep the topic at the margins, even while it was debated in the seminaries and in the colleges and universities.

The second development was much more important, and harder to handle. An innovative approach to the Bible developed in German universities known as the Higher Criticism threated to weaken the authority of revelation, the very standard by which evolution was problematic. By the early nineteenth century, breakthroughs in archaeology and philology showed that each snippet of the Bible had been composed under specific conditions. The book of Genesis, it turned out, was cobbled together from as many as four documents, written during different phases in the consolidation of the ancient Hebrews as a single people. The book of Isaiah was written by at least two authors living centuries apart. This new historical-critical approach was also applied to the New Testament. The letters of the Apostle Paul were designed to meet particular needs and circumstances, which needed to be taken into account in order to understand their true meaning. Some of the letters were not even written by Paul. Ephesians and Hebrews were the work of unknown authors. This study of the historical origins of texts, including the linguistic, archaeological, and cultural conditions, was called the Higher Criticism to distinguish it from Lower Criticism, which referred to the physical piecing together of the early manuscripts that had been recognized as biblical. Just as the Darwinian revolution embedded human beings directly into physical nature, so the Higher Criticism embedded the Holy Scriptures directly into human history. Even the soundest of faiths was developed by real people living in real time.

Justifiably fearful of how the people in their pews might react to this apparent diminution of the supernatural authority of the Bible, most preachers avoided talking about the actual history of the scriptures. President Grover Cleveland voiced a common sentiment: "The Bible is good enough for me: just the old book under which I was brought up. I do not want notes or criticism, or explanations about authorship or origin or even cross-references. I do not need them, and they confuse me."[6] The Unitarian minister and transcendentalist thinker Theodore Parker was unusual for writing extensively in a higher critical mode before the Civil War. The seminaries paid increasing but cautious attention to it later, during the last third of the nineteenth century. A historical perspective on the Bible was a delicate topic for nearly all of American Protestantism all the way to the end of the nineteenth century and beyond.

Even in the practice of science, where church members had less authority, Christian commitment influenced perspectives on evolution and on biblical scholarship. American scholars did not need the policing of church members to make them loyal to the faith, at least in its liberal constructions. The great majority of American scientists resisted natural selection as the sole mechanism of evolution, preferring an emphasis on the heritability of characteristics acquired during an organism's lifetime and making more room for divine supervision of the process. This "Lamarckian" school of evolutionary science, named for the French naturalist Jean-Baptiste Lamarck, came to be known in European circles as the "American school." The random character of species change as described by Darwin offended the persistent faith that a benevolent deity oversaw the whole process. The popularity down through the early twentieth century of this less rigorously naturalistic version of evolution marked the enduring authority of Protestantism even within the community of American scientists.

In America, as historian Henry F. May established, the Enlightenment took place largely within Protestantism rather than as a critique of it.[7] In Western Europe, by contrast, the critical spirit of the Enlightenment often took form as a critique of religion. Spinoza, Voltaire, and Hume exemplified this sensibility in the eighteenth century, followed in the nineteenth by Feuerbach, Mill, and Marx. But nineteenth-century America never developed anything comparable to the famous Victorian cohort of British free thinkers that included Mill, George Eliot, T. H. Huxley, John Tyndall, and W. K. Clifford.

The greatest rationalist voices in antebellum America were the Unitarian divines Parker and William Ellery Channing. Scorned or forgotten was Thomas Paine, whose radicalism was still part of the conversation at the time of the American Revolution. The transcendentalist philosophy of Ralph Waldo Emerson, by contrast, allowed plenty of room for God. Margaret Fuller, an even bolder, more radical thinker than Emerson, always remained loosely connected to her natal Unitarianism. An important exception was the pugnacious agnostic Robert Ingersoll, but even in the late nineteenth century great, freethinking orators never gained the respectability in America that their British counterparts did in their country.

A clear indication of what had happened to the Enlightenment in nineteenth-century America appeared in 1896 with the publication of *A History of the Warfare of Science with Theology in Christendom*. This formidable tome was written by Andrew Dickson White, a figure of national stature who was president of Cornell University and a former US ambassador to Russia. A devoted Episcopalian layman, White explained that the great conflict of modern times took place *within* "Christendom," where good, liberal Christians fought off the bad Christians who fell afoul of the theological dogmatism that prevented people from appreciating the advances of science.[8] Written explicitly to refute the popular concern that religion and science were in conflict, White's thesis registered the Protestantization of the Enlightenment in the United States.

By the time White exemplified the American intelligentsia's tendency to shelter Christianity from the more skeptical scrutiny it received in Western Europe, a liberalized Protestantism was largely in place in America's extensive system of private and public higher education. This was true in 1900 at the most distinguished of the new public universities, including Michigan, Wisconsin, Illinois, and California. Religion was more upfront at the leading private universities, especially at those that had been founded and sustained by the major denominations, including Yale (Congregationalist), Columbia (Episcopalian), Princeton (Presbyterian), Brown (Baptist), and Northwestern (Methodist). In 1892 the religiously serious Baptist John D. Rockefeller chose an eminent biblical scholar, William Rainey Harper, as the first president of the greatest of the new, nonsectarian universities, the University of Chicago. Even on that campus, enlightened religion and Wissenschaft lived quite comfortably together.

Beyond these cosmopolitan campuses, private and public, hundreds of denominationally focused, regional colleges educated many more Americans than did the universities. As late as 1900, college education was still a rarity in the United States. Only about 2 percent of Americans between the ages of eighteen and twenty-four were enrolled, but more than half of these attended church-related liberal arts colleges.[9] Not all confessions were equally committed to higher education, but the Presbyterians, Quakers, Congregationalists, Lutherans, and Methodists planted their own colleges wherever they had a substantial number of churches. The Methodists, for example, established a string of "Wesleyans" all over the middle section of the country. Ohio Wesleyan and Iowa Wesleyan were both founded in 1842, Illinois Wesleyan in 1850, and Kentucky Wesleyan in 1858, followed after the Civil War by several others, including Kansas Wesleyan (1886) and Nebraska Wesleyan (1887). These colleges exist to this day, as do many of the colleges founded by the various Lutheran synods, including Gettysburg (1832), Muhlenberg (1848), Augustana (1860), Luther (1861), St. Olaf (1874), Bethany (1881), and Pacific Lutheran (1890).

The standing and scope of education differed greatly by region, especially at the level of colleges and universities. The slaveholding elites of the pre–Civil War South were less committed to education than their socioeconomic counterparts in the rest of the nation. The Civil War's economic and social consequences then weakened what secondary education there had been and created further obstacles to the building of substantial postsecondary educational systems. The Confederate states were excluded from the Morrill Act of 1862, which provided funding for public universities and gave unprecedented impetus to higher education. At the end of the nineteenth century, none of the southern states had developed public universities comparable to those of Michigan, Wisconsin, Illinois, and

California. Even the University of Virginia, founded by Thomas Jefferson, did not become a major player in the academic world until the second half of the twentieth century.

Of the private universities that had emerged in America as centers of academic distinction by 1900, only Johns Hopkins was in a former slave state, and Maryland never joined the Confederacy. In the late twentieth century a number of southern states built strong public universities and many religiously affiliated colleges and universities (especially Methodist-sponsored Duke, Emory, and Vanderbilt). But these regional differences persisted and help to explain the enduring appeal of evangelical Protestantism to southern populations. As late as 1970, 18 percent of pastors of congregations affiliated with the Southern Baptist Convention had no schooling beyond high school.[10]

Differences in education contributed to a division between two families of Protestants that persisted throughout the twentieth century and became more important than ever in the twenty-first. In what historian Martin E. Marty called American Protestantism's informal "two-party system," one cluster of Protestants focused on individual salvation and personal morality, while another "lost faith in revivalism and worked instead . . . for some transformation of the world."[11] The first party was adamant that it understood an unchanging gospel literally, while the second was more willing to grant that people read the Bible in the light of worldly experience. The first party eventually fostered the Fundamentalist movement and a great variety of Pentecostal and Holiness churches that were unconnected to the traditional denominations, while the second flowered in the Social Gospel and Modernist movements.

Richard Hofstadter, in his classic study of 1964, ascribed to the revivalist-evangelical tradition "a one-hundred per cent mentality—a mind totally committed to the full range of the dominant popular fatuities and determined [to] tolerate no ambiguities, no equivocations, no reservations, and no criticism."[12] Later scholars have agreed that millions of Americans welcomed the firm biblical guidance the revivalist preachers claimed to offer. "In a world where violence, cheating, and unrest were common," notes Amanda Porterfield, "appeals to the authority of the Bible and punishments for sin proved more effective means of discipline" in many communities than did "appeals to the rational nature of mankind."[13] Most denominations were home to adherents of both parties, although the Unitarians and Episcopalians were always aloof from revivalism. After World War II, the two-party system became the ecumenical-evangelical divide, flagged by the two prominent magazines, the *Christian Century* and *Christianity Today*, and by two transdenominational organizations, the National Council of Churches and the National Association of Evangelicals.

Protestantism's two-party system developed independently of the two-party system of electoral politics. Federalists, Jeffersonians, Whigs, Republicans, and Democrats were from time to time more favored than not by members of one Protestant party or another. Just as the electoral two-party system shifted in ideological emphasis over the decades while remaining binary—consider how different the Republican Party of today is from what it was in Lincoln's time—so, too, did the two-party Protestant system experience pushes and pulls in different directions. The two kinds of Protestants sometimes engaged one another directly, but in many locations simply coexisted, practicing their own versions of the faith and quietly feeling superior to their neighbors.

Although both Protestant parties had vibrant constituencies in every section of the nation, there were striking regional variations. At the time of the Civil War, many northerners of both parties were antislavery, but southern whites—three-quarters of whom were on the revivalist-evangelical side of the religious divide—"believed," as one historian has explained, "that they were living in a Christian society precisely *because* they upheld the institution of slavery."[14] In the post–Civil War era, evangelicalism deepened its hold on the majority of southern whites. Both families flourished in the northern states following the war, but the liberals were able to strengthen their control over the denominations from which the more conservative southerners had departed in defense of slavery. Not until 1939 did the northern Methodists compromise their relative liberalism in order to unite again with their southern kin, at the significant cost of administratively segregating predominantly Black congregations, and not until 1983 did the northern and southern Presbyterians unite again. The yet more conservative Southern Baptists never rejoined their northern siblings.

For all their differences, the two families formed a single eth-noreligious tribe that inherited—and until relatively recently was committed to—the mission of helping their shared country achieve a Christian destiny, however differently they construed that goal. Not every empowered American was a white Protestant, but most of the people in control of social institutions were, and they assumed the same of each other, whether associated with tent meetings or with enlightened lecture halls.

William Jennings Bryan's "cross of gold" speech of 1896 worked so well because the scripture-centered Nebraska politician caught the connection between Jesus and the American population perfectly: "You shall not press down upon the brow of labor this crown of thorns, you shall not crucify mankind upon a cross of gold." President William McKinley thought and spoke conventionally when he concluded prayerfully in 1898 that Christian duty entailed his taking of the Philippines. When President Woodrow Wilson propelled the nation into global leadership in 1917, the connection between Christianity's missionary impulse and that of the secular American nation was obvious. When Wilson's rival, Theodore Roosevelt, shouted in a campaign speech of 1912, "We stand at Armageddon and we battle for the Lord," he spoke in keeping with popular understandings of religion and nationality. Even Elizabeth Cady Stanton, the freethinking feminist who rejected vast portions of the Bible as misogynist, spoke casually of "our Protestant" outlook on life.

This Anglo-Protestant tribe ran the country for a very long time. Even as late as 1960, someone in the upper echelons of any of the three branches of government, or otherwise in a position to influence the direction of society, was more likely than not— there were exceptions of course—to be at least nominally affiliated with a church belonging to one of the classic denominations: Methodists, Congregationalists, Presbyterians, Episcopalians, Disciples, Lutherans, Reformed, Unitarians, Baptists, and Quakers.

By 1960, however, ethnoreligious diversification had made the country more responsive to inclusive notions of community and more welcoming of the critical approaches to the world being advanced elsewhere in the wake of the Enlightenment. Diversity challenged the hegemony of a generic Protestantism and placed the old "Protestant establishment" on the edge of what turned out to be its precipitous decline after 1960.

Two changes in the ethnoreligious demography of the nation, taken up in the next two chapters, facilitated this opening up of public life. One was Jewish immigration. No other modern nation experienced Jewish immigration on the American scale, and no other immigrant-receiving national population was so thoroughly dominated by Protestants before the arrival of Jews. Jewish immigrants and their descendants confronted the well-established Protestants with something genuinely new: a substantial body of American citizens who achieved rapid upward class mobility and cultural influence but did not share a Christian background at all. The second change in eth-noreligious demography took place by long distance: Protes-tant missionaries and their children engaged non-Christian peoples face-to-face and for long periods of time, then returned home as vigorous critics of American cultural and religious pa-rochialism. Insistently and persistently, missionary-connected Americans bore witness to the humanity of non-Christian and nonwhite peoples. Adherents of non-Christian faiths were not "heathens," according to this relatively novel line of thought, but were "brothers and sisters." The missionaries expanded the scope of factual knowledge about the world and also achieved a substantial measure of "sentimental education," enabling greater empathic identification with previously exotic peoples.

Other influences, too, opened up a world beyond even the most capacious varieties of Protestantism. Urbanization put more Americans in contact with each other than before. Non-Jewish immigrants, especially Catholics, made society even more diverse. The rapid increase of secondary education from the Progressive Era onward made millions of Americans more aware of life beyond their own communities. Radio, motion pictures, and the greater circulation of national magazines from the 1920s onward brought more of the world into popular con-sciousness. The enlarged role of the "foreign correspondent" made a striking difference in what readers of newspapers learned about how lives were lived abroad. The rise of the United States as a power in international affairs also had a deprovincializing effect. Both world wars diminished ignorance of the breadth and complexity of the globe. The decolonization of the Global South after World War II made it harder to remain unaware of how small a percentage of the world was constituted by Anglo-Protestants.

All of these developments are well known and have been extensively studied. They would have diminished Protestant cultural hegemony even without substantial Jewish immigration, and even if missionaries had not campaigned against American cultural provinciality. But none of these other developments, with the exception of Catholic immigration, is ethnoreligiously defined. Jewish and missionary cosmopolitanism affected Christianity's place in the United States more directly. Each of these two cosmopolitanisms had its greatest impact, moreover, during the interregnum between the Johnson-Reed Act's ending of large-scale immigration in 1924 and the return of massive immigration in the 1970s following the Hart-Celler Act of 1965. That interregnum was a unique period of American history, during which the lack of massive immigration rendered Jewish and missionary diversifying influences all the more important.

Neither of these two influences has been sufficiently incorporated into either academic or popular narratives of the twentieth century. The Jewish impact has been recognized as important only within the subfield of American Jewish history and sometimes within intellectual history. Missionary cosmopolitanism, when recognized at all, has been treated almost exclusively within the subfield of American religious history. But each episode broadened the cultural horizons of millions of Americans.

Other non-Christian peoples were part of the country, too, but did not seriously threaten Protestant cultural hegemony. The Indigenous population that survived genocide was kept at a distance through the reservation system. Enslaved Africans brought their own religions with them, but they were not in a social position to challenge the ruling white Protestants, and eventually most of their descendants became Protestants themselves. Once that happened, African American Protestants threatened white supremacy in every national arena where they could make themselves known, including within the edifice of American Christianity. But the white Protestants of both major families proved capable of ignoring the interests and creativity of Black people, much more often than not, until well into the twentieth century. Thereafter, African American Protestants challenged and greatly broadened the ecumenical family and shamed the evangelical family for its slower response to their presence as Christians, as Americans, and as human beings.

3

Jewish Immigrants versus Anglo-Protestant Hegemony

Spinoza's ethics were no longer the Jewish ethics, but the ethics of man at large—just as his God was no longer the Jewish God: his God, merged with nature, shed his separate and distinctive divine identity. Yet, in a way, Spinoza's God and ethics were still Jewish, except that his Jewish monotheism carried to its logical conclusion and the Jewish universal God thought out to the end; and once thought out to the end, that God ceased to be Jewish.

—ISAAC DEUTSCHER, 1958

HANNAH ARENDT, Kenneth Arrow, Daniel Bell, Saul Bellow, Jack Benny, Milton Berle, Leonard Bernstein, Harold Bloom, Daniel Boorstin, Louis Brandeis, Joyce Brothers, Stanley Cavell, Noam Chomsky, Bob Dylan, Albert Einstein, Jason Epstein, Leslie Fiedler, Abraham Flexner, Jerome Frank, Felix Frankfurter, Betty Friedan, Milton Friedman, George Gershwin, Allen Ginsberg, Ruth Bader Ginsburg, Todd Gitlin, Nathan Glazer, Samuel Goldwyn, Paul Goodman, Clement Greenberg,

Peggy Guggenheim, Oscar Hammerstein, Oscar Handlin, Louis Hartz, Joseph Heller, Lillian Hellman, Will Herberg, Abraham Heschel, Richard Hofstadter, Sidney Hook, Irving Howe, Jacob Javits, Pauline Kael, Elena Kagan, Alfred Kazin, Henry Kissinger, Thomas Kuhn, Norman Mailer, Groucho Marx, Louis B. Mayer, Robert K. Merton, Thomas Nagel, Louise Nevelson, J. Robert Oppenheimer, Ayn Rand, David Riesman, Richard Rodgers, Sigmund Romberg, Julius Rosenwald, Walt Rostow, Philip Roth, Carl Sagan, Jonas Salk, Paul Samuelson, Bernie Sanders, Beverly Sills, Peter Singer, Susan Sontag, I. F. Stone, Barbra Streisand, Irving Thalberg, Lionel Trilling, Jack Warner, Ruth Westheimer, Stephen Wise, Janet Yellen.

Every person on this list of culturally prominent Americans was born to at least one Jewish parent, and in most cases two, and thus, no matter what their personal intentions, participated in a demographic challenge to Protestant cultural hegemony. The encounter of a Protestant culture with Jewish immigrants and their descendants, religious and secular, has been a pivotal event in the modern history of the United States.[1] Both of the two families of Protestant churches, ecumenical and evangelical, were confronted with this striking novelty. The idea of a "Christian America," widely shared in both families, was harder to maintain as non-Christians occupied more and more cultural space.

Exactly when did Jews have the greatest impact on public life? In what specific domains did Jews achieve leadership, and with what results? Where was Judaism, as opposed to Jewish ethnicity, important in the process of cultural change? Why is the story of Catholic immigrants and their descendants—who throughout most of the twentieth century were about six times as numerous—so different?

Jews were present in the colonial era of British North America but did not begin to diversify American society on a significant scale until a mid-nineteenth-century migration from German-speaking Central Europe. That episode was dwarfed by the massive immigration from Eastern Europe that began in the early 1880s and increased rapidly through the 1910s. Two million Jews entered the United States during those decades. A third, much smaller but highly distinctive wave of Jewish immigrants appeared in the 1930s, when scientists, writers, and artists were driven out Hitler's Europe.

Already by 1920 Jews constituted one-fifth of the population of New York City, even though they represented less than 4 percent of the national population. Since New York was the cultural and economic capital, the concentration of Jews there made them more significant players in public life than had they been widely distributed geographically. Jews were discriminated against in most institutional and social settings through the 1930s, but many managed to flourish in a variety of businesses, in labor unions, and in the service professions. Empowered Protestants encountered them regularly.

The upward social and economic mobility of Jews was enabled by several social characteristics that distinguished them from most other immigrants. Many Jews brought commercial experience and artisanal skills from the Old World. They also had a much higher rate of literacy than other immigrant groups. Jews were also more committed to making the United States a permanent home. About one-third of the non-Jewish immigrants of 1880–1920 actually returned to Europe, but Jews, many of whom were fleeing the pogroms of the Russian Empire, quickly put down roots in America and became as fully involved in public institutions as the Anglo-Protestant gatekeepers allowed.

These features of the immigrant experience distinguished Jews from most Catholic immigrants. Of the major Catholic ethnic groups, only the Irish, escaping the poverty of Ireland, were as likely as Jews to cross the Atlantic as families and to make America a permanent home from the time of their arrival. Polish and Italian immigrants were overwhelmingly male and often returned to their European homes after several years of employment in America. Moreover, few Catholic immigrants of any ethnicity were as literate as even impoverished Jewish immigrants, and few had as much commercial experience. The Eastern European Jews who arrived in the 1880s and after were also assisted by the philanthropies of the small but well-established population of German Jews who descended from the mid-nineteenth-century migration. Further, while some Catholic children attended public schools, many others went to parochial schools, which fostered a greater degree of social separation from the Anglo-Protestant majority. Finally, most Catholic priests were educated in Europe, while the immigrant Jewish community established schools to train their own Orthodox and Reform rabbis. These differences between Catholic and Jewish populations in the United States diminished over time, especially after Congress in 1917, and more decisively in 1924, cut off the immigration that kept Italian and Polish connections to Europe active. But by then the Jewish experience of upward mobility was well under way.

Congress's termination of large-scale immigration of Catholics and Jews in the 1920s played well with the majority of Anglo-Protestants. But a vocal minority disagreed. The Federal Council of Churches, dominated by Social Gospel Protestants, lobbied against anti-immigrant legislation and, after it had been enacted, worked unsuccessfully to reverse it. Beyond the churches, several leading figures in the legal profession, including US Supreme Court associate justice Oliver Wendell Holmes Jr., made a point of praising the intellectual power of Jewish lawyers and legal theorists. At the same historical moment, an outspoken group of young intellectuals based in New York's Greenwich Village welcomed Jews for the same reasons that the majority of Anglo-Protestants did not. These cultural radicals recognized the Jews they had come to know as instruments for diminishing the authority of what they regarded as flatulent pieties handed down from the Puritan and Victorian past. These poets, writers, and political activists celebrated Jews as agents of liberation, subverting outmoded ways of thinking.

The essays of the 1910s by the American progressive writer Randolph Bourne were emblematic of a number of cosmopolitan manifestos identifying Jewish immigrants as just what the United States needed to bring it into the modern world. "The intellectual service" to the country being delivered by young Jewish intellectuals, wrote Bourne, "can hardly be overvalued." What they are contributing "is so incomparably greater than that of any other American group of foreign affiliation that one can scarcely get one's perspective."[2] Hutchins Hapgood's *The Spirit of the Ghetto* (1909) encouraged his contemporaries to see the streets of New York's Lower East Side as filled with working-class Spinozas. Thorstein Veblen's "The Intellectual Preeminence of Jews in Modern Europe" (1919) credited Jews with a unique capacity for critical detachment highly functional in a modern, science-centered world.[3]

This domestic revolt against provincialism might not have been so confident and prolific had it not discovered and allied itself with a parallel movement of Jewish youth against the limited horizons of their own Eastern European heritage. The revolt against the shtetl had its own dynamic, but it dovetailed with the revolt against the Protestant village. Two autonomous antiprovincial initiatives connected and reinforced each other. Jewish youth eager to escape the constraints of Jewish

communal life absorbed Western learning with alacrity and passion. They interacted with Columbia University students like
Bourne, and with Greenwich Village writers like Hapgood and
Floyd Dell, who were just then proclaiming their annoyance
with the church-inflected culture they saw all around them.
H. L. Mencken's legendary attacks on "Puritanism" were typical
of this Anglo-Protestant spasm of annoyance.

The philosemitic engagements of Anglo-Protestants like
Bourne, Holmes, and the leaders of the Federal Council of
Churches are easily lost in a public memory that rightly emphasizes
the hostility displayed toward both Jewish and Catholic immigrants. Madison Grant's racist volume *The Passing of the Great Race*
(1916) was by far the most widely quoted document in the debates
leading up to Congress's curtailing of immigration in 1924.[4] Catholics and Jews were violently targeted by the Ku Klux Klan, along
with African Americans. Anti-Catholic attitudes had been common among Anglo-Protestants since well before the Civil War. The
Klan reinforced the idea that Catholics were pawns of Rome, a
foreign power. There is no question that the defenders of Protestant cultural hegemony won the political battles of the interwar
decades. Voices defending a more pluralist, inclusive America were
defeated at the time, but they demand our attention because they
were harbingers of a future in which Jewish immigrants helped to
inspire cosmopolitan strivings among Anglo-Protestants.

That future was accelerated by the arrival after 1933 of Jewish
scientists, scholars, writers, and artists escaping Hitler's Europe.
The federal government, lobbied by a host of private parties,
granted these exceptional individuals the opportunity to enter
the country, circumventing the prohibition enacted in 1924. The
illustrious newcomers made the Jewish presence in American
life more visible to everyone and a source of political pride in
the Hitler era. Albert Einstein was the most famous, but after

the Manhattan Project's work became widely known in 1945, the public became aware of the importance of a whole cohort of Jewish émigré physicists—including Edward Teller, Hans Bethe, and Leo Szilard. In the meantime, émigrés Hannah Arendt, Herbert Marcuse, and Franz Neumann and other social theorists were speaking to the desire for explanations of the rise of fascism. Elsewhere in academia and the arts, Billy Wilder, Albert Hirschman, Erwin Panofsky, Arnold Schoenberg, Ludwig von Mises, Kurt Weill, Hans Morgenthau, and Leo Strauss gained recognition for their achievements. Similarly, émigré psychologists and psychiatrists Erich Fromm, Erik Erikson, and Bruno Bettelheim played pivotal roles in the unprecedented popularization of psychology in the postwar era.

The refugee intellectuals were fully formed, established figures who brought with them the reputations they had made in Europe. Suddenly, Jews were much more heavily represented in the ranks of the most famous Americans than ever before. The 1931 edition of Who's Who reveals how novel this was. About fourteen thousand of the sixteen thousand Americans listed with a religious affiliation were Baptist, Congregationalist, Episcopalian, Methodist, Presbyterian, or Unitarian.[5] The Jewish émigrés of the Hitler era shattered the presumption of Anglo-Protestant cultural leadership.

The arrival of the refugee intellectuals, along with popular awareness of the European political context that brought them to the United States, dramatically improved the prospects of the pre-1924 Jewish immigrants and their offspring. American discriminatory practices against Jews were discredited by what had happened in Germany and by the constructions of American democracy that had been articulated during World War II. Anti-Semitic barriers to education, employment, and access to services could not survive.

The ending of discriminatory practices in higher education had stunning results because of the rapid expansion of universities during the postwar economic boom and the financing provided by the GI Bill. Jewish American academics who had been waiting for professional opportunities suddenly had them. Protestant tribal dominance diminished at the level of routine appointments of junior academics, not just for marque individuals arriving from Europe. Yale appointed its first Jew to the faculty of its undergraduate college in 1946, but less than a quarter century later about one-fifth of that faculty was Jewish.[6] The Carnegie Commission found that by the end of the 1960s, 17 percent of the faculties of the leading universities were Jewish. The opening of academia to Jews was especially apparent in disciplines relevant to public affairs: 36 percent of law professors, 34 percent of sociologists, 28 percent of economists, and 24 percent of political science professors on the most highly ranked campuses were Jewish.[7]

A closer look at the discipline of philosophy illustrates the de-Christianization of academia. Philosophy is an especially useful window on this process because it has been traditionally concerned with the place of religion in understanding the world.

Well before Jews entered the profession, some American philosophers of Protestant origin moved independently to challenge the old habit of sheltering Christian belief from skeptical questioning.[8] John Dewey, born in Vermont into a Congregationalist family in 1859, did not need a change in his ethnoreligious company in order to become, by the early twentieth century, an advocate for a science-driven philosophy. Yet in Dewey's time the discipline was still dominated by two intellectual giants who continued to protect Protestantism from serious epistemic challenges. William James's greatest work was titled *The Varieties of Religious Experience*, Josiah Royce's was called *The Problem of Christianity*.[9] The pragmatist James assured his large following that religion could survive scientific scrutiny. The idealist Royce developed an ambitious metaphysics organized around an all-seeing, all-powerful force he called "the Absolute," which he presented as fully consistent with the Apostle Paul's construction of the Christian faith. Hence some of the substance of Christianity had disappeared in the leading American philosophers, but its theistic frame and theologically inflected language remained largely in place. This was the context in which Dewey, Roy Wood Sellars, and other secularists wrote the "Humanist Manifesto" of 1933, taking direct aim at the persistence of Christianity in the intellectual life of the nation and even in the gradually secularizing but still Protestant-toned domain of academia.[10]

These secular philosophers of Anglo-Protestant origin were then joined by Jewish colleagues who eagerly engaged the latest work of British and Continental European thinkers that emerged from cultural settings in which there was no longer a habit of favoring religion of any kind. Yet because presidents and trustees of colleges and universities were reluctant to appoint Jews in what was recognized as a religiously relevant discipline, it took several decades for Jews to gain institutional standing. Prior to World War II, only one Jew was recognized as a leader in American academic philosophy. Morris R. Cohen had immigrated from Russia as a child in 1892 and was the first Jew to earn a doctorate in philosophy at Harvard University.[11] He taught at the City College of New York but was passed over for more prestigious appointments despite his obvious professional qualifications. By the early 1940s a handful of Jews had obtained philosophy appointments, but only during the postwar academic boom, accompanied by the end of anti-Semitic barriers, was the discipline's ethnoreligious demography transformed.

Once the transformation began, it was swift and sweeping. By the end of the 1960s, one in five of the members of the nation's leading philosophy departments was Jewish. A newspaper article of 1964 illustrates this and reveals how little it was remarked upon once it had taken place. In "How Today's Thinkers Serve Society," eight of the nation's most acclaimed professors of philosophy were invited to describe their work and its social contributions.[12] Each offered a few accessible paragraphs that, taken together, add up to a reasonably accurate summary of the almost entirely religion-free engagements of their discipline at that historical moment. Yet this article in the *National Observer* said nothing of the fact that seven of the eight, chosen apparently at random from the ranks of the recognized leaders of the discipline, were Jews. Only W. V. O. Quine was not. Four of the seven had been students of Cohen's at CCNY: Sidney Hook, Ernest Nagel, Paul Weiss, and Morton White. Three others were Max Black, Abraham Kaplan, and Walter Kaufmann, all of whom had arrived from Europe as children or youths. Less than twenty years after the end of World War II a journalist could work up a list of leading philosophers without thinking their ethnoreligious identities invited any mention at all.

Hook, Kaufmann, and White sometimes wrote skeptically about the intellectual claims of Christianity. Kaufmann made a stir in 1958 when he dismissed the philosophical capabilities of the most popular theologian of the era, Reinhold Niebuhr. "Occasionally hailed as America's greatest thinker," Kaufmann scoffed, "he has not made his mark as a scholar," and his crude apologetic writings prove he can read scripture only as a mirror of his own ideas.[13] But what mattered more was something less direct and immediate: the simple shifting of the discipline's center of gravity away from theories of knowledge, of the world, and of morality in which a God recognizable to Protestants was an even passive presence. The non-Jewish Quine voiced this consensus, insisting that philosophy of science was the only philosophy needed. The discipline that had been one of the most attentive to Christianity had become one of the least.

In that respect the discipline of philosophy was merely an unusually explicit case of a general transferal of cultural authority from religion to Wissenschaft. "Religion had to go," writes a sociologist, because "a continuing influence of the Protestant establishment" in higher education, science, and literature "would restrict the potential autonomy, status, and authority of . . . aspiring knowledge elites."[14]

In 1960 Princeton University president Robert F. Goheen characterized this de-Christianization as a basic reality in "most of the realms of culture for which the university takes responsibility." Those realms "have attained a variety and maturity which require that the worldly pursuit of learning in them be free from explicit connection with the enterprise of religion and theology."[15] This academic emancipation did not result solely from the presence of Jewish intellectuals, but without them the transformation would have been slower and less decisive.

Beyond academia, Jewish clinical psychologists, social workers, and psychiatrists were prominent players in the process by which ministers were gradually replaced by mental health professionals as authorities for dealing with personal problems. One did not have to be Jewish to appreciate the value of psychotherapy, but Jewish clinicians were heavily overrepresented in the mental health professions in the United States during the midcentury decades. And psychoanalysis, one of the major approaches to therapy, had been invented by a Jewish atheist who treated religion as a form of superstition.

This displacement of the clergy by therapists relying on secular methods, rather than the application of church doctrine, took place quietly. It was almost never advanced as an explicitly secularizing project. Regular churchgoers, while respecting their ministers, relied on clerical authority for less than their parents and grandparents did. Often, the clinicians themselves were former preachers who regarded the change in vocation as consistent with the values they had espoused from the pulpit and in "pastoral counseling."

The switch made sense to ministers who found that the anxieties, depressions, and marital problems brought to them by their parishioners were best dealt with through therapy. Prayer and biblical precepts were not abandoned, but they were not enough. The dilemmas parishioners shared with their ministers were "no longer signs of God's word, or occasions for thinking about ultimate reality," notes scholar Andrew Abbott, but immediate social and emotional events driven by the opportunities and constraints of contemporary culture. The displacement took place, Abbott adds, not so much through the aggression of nonclerical analysts and therapists but through "the clergy's willful desertion of its traditional work."[16]

Several of the most influential of the midcentury's clinical psychologists, including Carl Rogers and Rollo May, had begun their own careers as Protestant ministers. The "gospel of clinical psychology," as it was sometimes characterized sardonically, became widespread in the 1950s. It took institutional form in many ecumenical congregations. Roy Burkhardt's huge Congregational church in Columbus, Ohio, operated its own clinic and supervised a national network of "Burkhardt Seminars" popularizing the practice. Although Freud was a powerful influence on many of the preachers-turned-therapists, more were attracted instead to the "self-realization" psychology developed by the "humanistic" school led by Rogers, May, and Abraham Maslow, another Jewish intellectual who influenced modern American culture. "Self-realization could be discussed and marketed," as historian Edwin S. Gaustad observed, "quite apart from the Christian religion."[17] So, too, could psychoanalysis.

In many other public arenas, Jewish Americans achieved leadership. In literary culture, the popularity of Jewish novelists—especially Saul Bellow, Norman Mailer, Joseph Heller, and J. D. Salinger—led critic Leslie Fiedler in 1967 to hail "the great take-over by Jewish American writers . . . of the task of dreaming aloud the dreams of the whole American people," a task inherited "from certain Gentile predecessors, urban Anglo-Saxons and Midwestern provincials of North European origin."[18] In Hollywood, the film industry from the 1920s through the 1960s was largely run by the sons of Eastern European Jewish immigrants whose movies invited the public to behold an idealized America generic enough to accommodate highly assimilated Jews like themselves. Matinee idols, whatever their own ethnicity, were designed to be accessible to all white Americans, not to serve as accurate mirrors of subgroup particularism. James Stewart, Gary Cooper, Ginger Rogers, Clark Gable, Lauren Bacall, Cary Grant, and Ava Gardner inhabited a world in which, as Neal Gabler explains, "fathers were strong, families stable, people attractive, resilient, resourceful, and decent." This "invention" of the Jewish lords of Hollywood, Gabler remarks, "may be their most enduring legacy."[19]

The US Senate had no Jewish members in 1949, but thirty years later there were ten. By the end of the 1970s, nearly 40 percent of the partners in the leading law firms of New York and Washington were Jewish, as were about a quarter of the reporters, editors, and executives of the major print and broadcasting media.[20] Secular Jewish men and women made up approximately one-third of the young white participants in the Mississippi Summer voting rights campaign of 1964.[21] Nearly all of the recognized leaders of "second-wave feminism" in the 1960s and 1970s were secular Jewish women. These included Bella Abzug, Susan Brownmiller, Andrea Dworkin, Shulamith Firestone, Betty Friedan, Vivian Gornick, Florence Howe, Gerda Lerner, Robin Morgan, Letty Cottin Pogrebin, Alix Kates Schulman, Gloria Steinem, Meredith Tax, Naomi Weisstein, and Ellen Willis. Indeed, very few of the recognized feminist leaders of that generation were not Jewish. Mary Daly, bell hooks, and Kate Millett were unusual in that respect.

These Jewish feminists, historian Joyce Antler notes, almost never proclaimed Jewish identity. They understood their political and cultural labors in a universalist framework. "They refrained from explicitly asserting that ancestral inheritances drove the momentum for change." Antler observes that this preference for universal over particular identities was in itself an ancestral inheritance, however, since Jews had so long been treated unfairly on ethnoracially particularistic grounds.[22]

The secular orientation of the Jewish feminists exemplified one of two ways in which Jews contributed to the decline of Anglo-Protestant cultural hegemony. The other was the greater acceptance of Judaism, which was central to the celebration of the "Judeo-Christian tradition." This concept was not new to the Cold War era, but it was then widely affirmed as part of the struggle of the United States against "godless communism." A number of Protestant theologians, Catholic priests, and Jewish rabbis participated in this celebration of a "tri-faith America," hailed as an inclusive step, repudiating the anti-Catholic and anti-Semitic elements in the national past. In a best-selling

book of 1955, *Protestant-Catholic-Jew: An Essay in Religious Sociology*, Will Herberg popularized this elevation of Catholicism and Judaism as symbolically equal partners in defining American life.[23]

But the popularization of a Judeo-Christian America was no more a Jewish project than a Catholic and Protestant one. It could not have happened without a strong Jewish presence in public life, but Catholic and Protestant leaders had their own reasons for welcoming the representation of Jews as Judaic. Early in the Cold War, the Catholic hierarchy pivoted toward ever-more adamant anti-Soviet postures, putting behind them the display of sympathy for fascist regimes in Italy and Spain that had been common prior to the American entry into World War II. Protestants like Reinhold Niebuhr, worried about secularization, were glad to have a religious conception of the United States affirmed.

The "Judeo-Christian tradition" welcomed Jews only in their capacity as children of the Old Testament. A tri-faith America made no provision for Jews who were not religious. The dynamic, as K. Healan Gaston has documented, was one of exclusion as well as inclusion.[24] Moreover, the Judeo-Christian model for American life excluded Americans who had departed from an ancestral Catholicism or Protestantism. The concept of a Judeo-Christian America, while popular with many ecumenical Protestant leaders who saw it as consistent with their liberalizing goals, projected an America that was de-Christianized only to become more inclusively biblical. The potentially secularizing force of the Jewish population was partly neutralized by Judaizing it, incorporating it into a religiously defined nation.

Considered as an affirmation of religious pluralism, the notion of a Judeo-Christian America obscured the more thoroughly secular versions of de-Christianization that were well under way. The great majority of ethnic Jews who exercised leadership in public arenas were not conspicuously Judaic, whatever their measure of personal interest in Judaism. They contributed to an ethos in which religious identity mattered less, not more. Indeed, Jews were more likely to have drifted away from their natal religion than their contemporaries who had grown up in Catholic or Protestant churches. The Carnegie Commission's study of the American professorate at the end of the 1960s revealed that among faculty in colleges and universities, those from Jewish families were about twice as likely as those from Protestant or Catholic families to say they had abandoned the religion of their natal community. At the most prestigious universities, 72 percent of the ethnically Jewish faculty represented themselves as having no religion at all.[25] Nearly all of the Hitler-era refugee intellectuals were aloof from religion.

Secular and religious Jews were important players in mid-twentieth-century efforts to sharpen church-state separation. As the most conspicuously non-Christian group in the country, Jews enhanced the credibility of several organizations lobbying for a more strictly secular civic sphere, free of any religious sectarianism and free, in particular, of implications that the United States was a nation of Christians. The American Civil Liberties Union and other secular organizations had been spearheading this litigation during the 1920s and 1930s. They were joined in the early 1940s by the American Jewish Committee and other Jewish organizations, whose attorneys—especially Leo Pfeiffer—became central to the separationists' campaign. Primarily at issue in a series of suits Pfeiffer and his colleagues brought was how much the non-establishment clause of the First Amendment restricted the use of public funds for any kind religious instruction.[26] Many pains were taken ensure that few of the plaintiffs in church-state litigation carried Jewish names.[27] To make the Jewish organizations feel more comfortable, Pfeffer hired an Episcopalian lawyer to be the public face of a 1952 suit. Names that conveyed a presumption of Protestantism were preferred. Were Jews helping to make the United States a less Christian country? Of course they were. But this was a dangerous truth. Advocates of stronger church-state separation knew better than to trumpet it.

Worries about "Jewish influence" existed long before the Jewish involvement in church-state litigation and remained alive long after the litigation of the midcentury decades. In what became a widely quoted example, Billy Graham once joined President Richard Nixon in complaining about Jewish influence. Both chatted about this candidly in 1972, while accepting Nixon's observation that neither of them could say such things in public. Graham warned against a Jewish "stranglehold" that "has got to be broken or the country's going down the drain." The famous preacher added, without prompting, that if Nixon were to be reelected, "we might be able to do something" about it. When tapes of this conversation were made public in 2002, Graham apologized. But there is no reason to doubt his sincerity at the time, nor to suppose this was the only time Graham spoke in this manner, distant, of course, from recording devices. When given a chance to challenge Nixon's anti-Semitic opinions, the evangelist at the height of his prestige and authority instead endorsed them and volunteered that his own Jewish friends, while flattering him, "don't know how I really feel about what they are doing to this country."[28]

What were Jews "doing to the country"?

Irving Berlin's songs "White Christmas" and "Easter Parade" popularized an entirely de-Christianized image of and a secular point of access to the most sacred Christian holidays. Bing

Crosby's 1942 recording of Berlin's nostalgic, highly sentimental "White Christmas" was an immediate hit and remains the biggest-selling single record of all time.[29] The Jewish songwriter was not attacking Christians, but he was rendering the holiday safe for every American. Philip Roth gave the point an ironic and mocking twist that would probably have puzzled Berlin. "God gave Moses the Ten Commandments and then He gave Irving Berlin 'Easter Parade' and 'White Christmas,'" Roth wrote in *Operation Shylock: A Confession*. "The two holidays that celebrate the divinity of Christ—the divinity that's the very heart of the Jewish rejection of Christianity—and what does Irving Berlin brilliantly do? He de-Christs them both! Easter he turns into a fashion show and Christmas into a holiday about snow."[30]

Roth's fantasy about Jews slipping unnoticed into Anglo-Protestant American life was belied, as he well knew, by sentiments like Graham's and Nixon's, even if rarely expressed outright. T. S. Eliot did not mind saying them out loud: "free thinking Jews" threatened America. In his notorious 1934 defense of religious and racial uniformity, Eliot declared that "the population should be homogeneous." What is "still more important," the great poet told an audience of Virginians, and later the entire English-speaking world in his book *After Strange Gods*, "is unity of religious background." Eliot continued, more explicitly: "Reasons of race and religion combine to make any large number of free-thinking Jews undesirable."[31] Yet, gradually, the people Eliot had in mind did exactly what he feared they would do: they diversified the United States. They made it more difficult to maintain the old habits of sheltering Christianity's epistemic claims from modern scientific interrogation and of uncritically accepting Christianity as the spiritual frame for American national destiny.

4

The Missionary Boomerang

Jesus is ideal and wonderful, but you Christians, you are not
like him.

—DANA TAGORE, ABOUT 1910

ONE DAY in 1923, John R. Mott, the undisputed leader of American Protestant missionary efforts throughout the world, spent
the morning with former president William Howard Taft, who
was then chief justice of the US Supreme Court. Mott then
went to the White House for lunch with President Calvin Coo-
lidge. In the afternoon, Mott called on his old friend, the ailing
former president, Woodrow Wilson.[1] Three presidents in one
day. Mott's social calendar reveals the public standing of missionaries a hundred years ago.

In 1925 there were ten thousand American missionaries
abroad, primarily in China, Japan, Korea, the Middle East, and
India, but also distributed elsewhere across the globe beyond the
North Atlantic West. The cultural role of missionaries was much
greater than their numbers would imply. To be a missionary was
to have accepted a challenging and honored calling. The missionaries sent out by the major denominations were anything

but marginal, socially. Often they were graduates of Princeton, Yale, Oberlin, Mount Holyoke, or Amherst. Missionaries were in the vanguard, taking risks to advance what were understood as the finest features of American society, spreading them out to the wider world. They were the bullfighters of Protestantism.

From the start of the American Protestant foreign missionary project in the 1830s, secular as well as religious magazines reported extensively on missionary activities. The size and social prominence of the missionary project grew rapidly in the 1880s and 1890s. By the early twentieth century, the organizations sponsoring the project were among the largest and most influential voluntary associations in the United States. Some missionary leaders held important positions in the federal government, especially during the Wilson administration. Quite a few were on relaxed social terms with the most powerful businessmen in the country, including Cleveland Dodge and John D. Rockefeller Jr. Some missionary leaders were guests at Rockefeller's summer home on Mount Desert Island, Maine.

Missionaries were insiders to America and to Christianity. As such, they were different from Jewish immigrants. They differed also in the parts of the globe with which they were engaged. When Jewish immigrants and their descendants looked abroad, they focused on Europe. When missionaries and their children and their supporting organizations looked beyond the United States, they were inspired by Asia, and to some extent by Latin America, Africa, and the South Pacific. Jewish cosmopolitanism and missionary cosmopolitanism ran parallel to one another, but they expanded American horizons in different directions and almost never took account of one another. Hence it is all the more important to understand each on its own terms.

What made the missionaries so critical of American provinciality? In what areas of public life was their influence registered? How did missionary cosmopolitanism affect the Protestant churches? How did missionary perspectives on religion relate to race and ethnicity?

Mark Twain's sense that "travel is fatal to prejudice, bigotry, and narrow-mindedness" does not always apply.[2] But it did for thousands of missionaries. The experience of living with peoples really different from themselves, much to their surprise, changed their understandings of themselves, of their country, and of humanity. Missionaries were expected to make the rest of the world "more like us," more like American Protestants. But by the 1920s, a steady stream of missionary writings insisted that this old aspiration was a mistake.

The gospel ended up working like a boomerang, thrown across the sea but not staying there. It returned, carrying unexpected baggage.[3] The rest of humanity was more than a needy expanse, awaiting the benevolence and supervision of American Protestants. Many returning missionaries became informal ambassadors from foreign peoples to Americans and vocal advocates of tolerance and inclusion. Some missionaries, to be sure, fit the popular stereotype of defenders of imperialism and empire, scornful of indigenous cultures. The missionaries most likely to become cosmopolitan critics of American narrowness were the most educated: those who had attended liberal arts colleges and leading seminaries.

The mission field was an important battleground between ecumenical and evangelical missionaries. This was true from the start and remained a prominent reality of the American missionary endeavor. One scholar found that even as late as the 1960s, "the most urgent issue facing Protestantism in the Congo" for evangelical missionaries was "the power of ecumenical Christianity, not traditional religion."[4]

Evangelicals, like ecumenicals, had global reach, but the ecumenically minded missionaries were much quicker to change their inherited ideas. In the major denominations, the tone of missionary representation of foreign peoples moved steadily away from invidious language and toward the universalist vision of Galatians 3:28: "There is neither Jew nor Gentile, neither slave nor free, nor is there male and female, for you are all one in Christ Jesus." Ecumenical missionaries also differed from evangelical missionaries in their postmission role in American public life. The evangelicals, even when liberalized by their experience abroad, almost never became State Department officers, Ivy League professors, best-selling authors, or leaders of social reform movements. They did become prominent within evangelical institutions, and there sometimes argued against ethnocentrism.[5]

The ecumenical missionary contingent included many who regarded the great Hindu leader Mohandas Gandhi—invariably called "Mahatma," for "great soul"—as the most fully Christian person in the world. His peace-loving, generous behavior showed what it would mean to "walk humbly in the Lord." Beyond Gandhi, Hindus, Muslims, Buddhists, and followers of other non-Christian faiths were no longer to be scorned as heathens or patronized as less than complete human beings. Rather, they were "brothers and sisters." God had made "all nations of one blood," according to Acts 17:26, a verse that came into more common use in the United States in the context of foreign missions.

The link between religious ecumenism and ethnoracial inclusion was a constant refrain of this liberalizing missionary discourse. The missionary-influenced church leaders of the

1930s promoted Japanese preacher Toyohiko Kagawa and showcased him as an example of how persons of a foreign race could exemplify and evangelize for the Christian faith just as well as any white man. In 1936 alone, Kagawa spoke in a hundred fifty American cities before audiences of seventy-five thousand. He was regularly attacked by fundamentalists, making the ecumenical leaders all the more devoted to Kagawa as a carrier of their universalist gospel.[6]

Protestants missionaries from European nations also popularized ecumenical and antiracist ideas, but the European missionaries operated in the context of colonial empires. The British, Dutch, and German missionaries and their churchgoing supporters were more familiar with foreign peoples and less struck by the missionary encounter with them. For American missionaries and their followers back home, sustained contact with the peoples of Asia, Africa, Latin America, and the South Seas was more novel than for their counterparts in Europe. The European missionary groups remained more comfortable with empire than the Americans, who proved highly responsive to decolonization when that world-changing process unfolded after World War II.

Business, military, and diplomatic connections abroad also promoted awareness of peoples beyond the North Atlantic West, as did *National Geographic* and the most popular works of anthropologists Margaret Mead and Ruth Benedict. But these secular reports on the wider world registered with a smaller segment of the public. Denominational periodicals delivered missionary testimony to American homes even in the most isolated locations. The missionary boomerang brought traces of radically different "others" directly into local churches and homes. Missionaries were intimate and trusted witnesses to world events. Missionaries on furlough were usually the featured speakers at national and regional denominational meetings and appeared regularly at Sunday night services in local churches. It was common for congregations to correspond for decades with specific missionary families to whose support they contributed financially. During the 1920s, some denominations allocated as much as 90 percent of their annual budget to foreign missions.[7]

Presbyterian missionary daughter Pearl Buck was perhaps the most acclaimed exemplar of missionary cosmopolitanism. Her 1931 novel *The Good Earth* portrayed Chinese men, women, and children in intimate terms that prompted American readers to empathize with them as if they were siblings. On her way to the Pulitzer and Nobel prizes, Buck inspired countless reviewers to remark on how familiar she had made Chinese peasants seem. The *Christian Century*'s reviewer marveled that the central character of *The Good Earth* would have been no different "spiritually" had he "toiled on the Nebraska prairie rather than China." Buck's characters were multidimensional, striving individuals, each with a distinctive personality, profoundly different from the stereotypical candidates for conversion and benevolence long featured in even the most generous of what Americans were accustomed to reading about China. Later generations found elements of Orientalism in *The Good Earth*, but Buck challenged Orientalist stereotypes more effectively than any other popular writer of her generation. Will Rogers, the Oklahoma cracker-barrel philosopher who then enjoyed a national audience, described *The Good Earth* as "not only the greatest book about a people ever written, but the best book of our generation." Historians of East-West cultural relations find that Buck altered Western perspectives on China more than anyone since Marco Polo.[8]

Buck's fiction of the 1940s and 1950s no longer won critical praise, yet many of her books were best sellers. Moreover, as one of the widely known and respected women in the country, Buck used her fame to become a public voice for a number of progressive causes. She advocated independence for India well before it was achieved, campaigned for the repeal of the Chinese Exclusion Act, and was a steadfast supporter of the National Association for the Advancement of Colored People. Walter White, the president of the NAACP, and other Black leaders could always count on Buck to support their programs while other white allies temporalized. As early as 1941, Buck demanded that women be given access to contraception and be paid salaries equal to those of men when performing the same labor. Buck articulated most of the ideas popularized two decades later by Betty Friedan's *The Feminine Mystique*, a book the then-aged Buck enthusiastically endorsed. Buck established and financed the first adoption agency specializing in transracial adoption. Buck was for "three decades," biographer Hilary Spurling summarizes, a campaigner "for peace, tolerance, and liberal democracy, for the rights of children and minorities, for an end to discrimination on grounds of race and gender."[9]

American writer and journalist John Hersey was also a "man for causes," many of them shared with Buck. But this China-born missionary son made his greatest mark by enabling the American public to see themselves in the lives of ordinary Japanese people. This achievement was all the more remarkable for its timing: only a year after the end of the American war against Japan. Hersey's detailed account of the experience of six survivors of the atomic bomb attack on the city of Hiroshima had much in common with Buck's novel about the Chinese. Hersey's poetic reportage enabled readers to experience a great range of emotions while recognizing the basic humanity of people who may well have been relatives of the Japanese soldiers whose depredations Americans had reason to condemn.

Hiroshima is a materially dense, highly naturalistic, and minutely described story of pain and desolation, told without moral reflection. There is no argument that dropping atomic bombs on Japan was a mistake, nor that it was a military necessity. There is no plea for abolishing atomic weapons.[10]

"The power of his text is not just a matter of its raw material," one literary scholar observed recently about *Hiroshima*. There is Hersey's "startling intimacy with the people he writes about: with poor, maddened Mr. Fukai, determined to break free of his rescuers and run back into the flames to die; with Dr. Sasaki, wearing the spectacles he has borrowed from a nurse, applying first aid to surviving patients."[11] The editors of the *New Yorker* devoted the entire August 31, 1946, issue to what Hersey then published as a book. Readers reported that they stopped everything to finish the article in silence. Albert Einstein reportedly ordered a thousand copies to distribute to people he thought should read it.

Ruth Benedict's *The Chrysanthemum and the Sword*, published in the same year as *Hiroshima*, also enabled Americans to recognize more humanity in the Japanese people than they had felt before. But Benedict wrote sweepingly about national traits, while Hersey, like Buck, wrote about specific individuals. Unlike Benedict's anthropological classic, which sold only twenty-eight thousand copies in twenty-five years, *Hiroshima* was a runaway best seller and has never dropped from view. In 1999 a panel of distinguished journalists identified it as the finest piece of journalistic writing in the twentieth century. Some of Hersey's other writings displayed the same capacity for empathic engagement with peoples far from the American heartland. *The Wall*, published in 1950, was the first novel to deal with the Holocaust and the first to use that word in print. The Yale and prep school graduate, a descendant of generations of

Congregationalists, was praised in *Commentary* and other Jewish magazines for his sensitive depiction of the society and culture of Polish Jewry.

Henry Luce, also a missionary child, was different, but only up to a point. Compared with Buck and Hersey, Luce was more conservative and very much more an American nationalist. But he used his influence as the publisher of *Time, Life,* and *Fortune* to promote attention to contemporary Asia. He put Chinese Nationalist leader Chiang Kai-shek on the cover of *Time* a dozen times. Chiang and his wife, the equally famous, media-savvy Madame Chiang, were both Christian converts, rendering them less striking departures than Gandhi as heroes for Americans to admire. Luce's magazines, especially *Life,* were consistently critical of racial discrimination well before other national periodicals had made that ideological turn.

Luce remained nominally Presbyterian, unlike Buck and Hersey, who both abandoned religion altogether. Nonetheless, Luce's "American Century" of 1941 recast the old Protestant call to change the world as a national project, not a Christian one. Luce's nationalism was less Christian than the internationalism of its most famous rebuttal, the leftist Henry Wallace's *The Century of the Common Man.*[12] Ironically, Luce's treatise was more genuinely cosmopolitan than anything the god-talking Wallace ever wrote.[13] The publisher's sense of what it meant to be an American, for all its national chauvinism, was neither as ethnocentric nor as religiously sectarian as that of his major leftist critic.

Luce was a leader of the liberal wing of the Republican Party and in that role knew Minnesota Republican congressman Walter Judd. A Congregationalist missionary doctor in China before being elected to Congress in 1942, Judd proved to be one of the most vigorously antiracist members of the House of

Representatives. He struggled for a decade to convince Congress to repeal of the "whites-only" provision of naturalization law that had been in place since 1790. Because the Thirteenth Amendment guaranteed citizenship for emancipated African Americans and the 1848 treaty ending the Mexican War promised naturalization to Mexican immigrants, the law's chief function was to deprive immigrants from Asia of the opportunity to become citizens. Judd tried to win support for the "Judd Bill," which floated in and out of committees, session after session of Congress. Finally it became law in 1952, when its contents—repeal of the whites-only regulation—were incorporated into the McCarran-Walter Act. Judd was the single person most responsible for this landmark event in the diminution of white supremacy's hold on American law.[14]

Missionary-connected Americans were also conspicuous in speaking out against the confinement of Japanese Americans during World War II. The missionary lobby protested this policy more swiftly, more persistently, and more loudly than any other identifiable group of white Americans. Anthropologists, then another strongly antiprovincial presence in American life, almost never opposed the US government's policies toward the Japanese Americans during the years when the missionary contingent's opposition was on public display. Missionary-connected authors castigated the policy in the *Christian Century*, the most prominent national magazine to oppose the government's action. Galen Fisher, a former missionary to Japan, led the largest of the organizations lobbying on behalf of the confined Japanese Americans. Pearl Buck pressed the issue directly with her personal friend, First Lady Eleanor Roosevelt. Former missionaries supervised the process whereby the Japanese Americans eventually released from Manzanar, Tule Lake, Minidoka, and other camps were placed in homes and jobs, often in locations distant from the Pacific Coast, where they had lived before the war.

Across the Pacific, former missionaries made another, highly distinctive mark on the World War II era. They saved thousands of Japanese POWs from violent abuse and death. Placed in charge of the interrogation of captured soldiers because of their exceptional facility with the Japanese language, the missionaries who accepted commissions in the Marine Corps, Army, and Navy proved that decent treatment of POWs produced more and better intelligence while displaying the most admirable features of American culture. In so doing, these officers defied superiors with traditional, racist views of the Japanese people. Marine Lt. Col. Sherwood Moran, who was part of the first wave at Guadalcanal, had spent twenty-six years as a Congregationalist missionary in Japan. He wrote an interrogation manual instructing all interrogators to treat the Japanese soldiers as "brothers."[15] In all three services active in the Pacific War, the missionary impact was the same, yet without any interservice cooperation. Service rivalries kept each service's programs for POW interrogation separate; only after the war was the independent power of the missionary witness on behalf of the Japanese soldiers recognized.

While what these military officers did during World War II was never widely known at the time, the Foreign Service was a setting in which the appreciation for foreign peoples was more visible. "China hands" John Paton Davies Jr. and John S. Service were purged in the McCarthy Era for their willingness during the war to engage the Chinese Communists. They warned the American government against too great a reliance on the patently corrupt Christian convert, Chiang Kai-shek. In policy debates about the Middle East, a substantial cohort of Beirut-born missionary sons fought against the anti-Arab prejudice that was widespread in the Department of State. One of these, William A. Eddy, was close enough to King Ibn Saud of Saudi Arabia to detach him from his traditional British allies and to connect him to the United States, including through the Dhahran air base for which Eddy was largely responsible. Eddy was so trusted by both the Saudis and the American government that he served as translator for both King Saud and President Roosevelt in an epochal meeting between the two in 1945 devoted to the volatile issue of Jewish settlement in Palestine. Eddy and his missionary colleagues then sought to convince the administrations of Truman and Eisenhower to view Arab nationalism and the Islamic religion in more sympathetic lights.

These missionary "Arabists" pursued a largely unsuccessful effort to get the US government to renounce the clients of the old European colonial empires still found in Egypt, Iraq, and other Middle Eastern countries. They understood the British government's Balfour Declaration of 1917 as an imperialist gambit, and they advised against the recognition of Israel in 1948 even while acknowledging that the Jewish state was a response to prejudice of a different sort, and on a massive scale. American policy toward Israel was the only issue on which missionary cosmopolitanism divided from Jewish cosmopolitanism, although some missionary-connected individuals and groups supported Truman's recognition of Israel, and some Jewish Americans opposed it. The missionary diplomats were aloof from the 1953 CIA coup replacing Mohammad Mosaddegh with the pro-Western Shah, and most of them opposed the landing of American troops in Lebanon in 1958. The American "missionary tradition," observed historian Hugh Milford, lost out during the Cold War to "the British imperial legacy" embraced by Dulles and Eisenhower.[16]

The most historically important of the missionary diplomats during and immediately after World War II designed and put into place the post–World War II alliance between Thailand and United States. As the only Foreign Service officer with any knowledge of Southeast Asia, Kenneth Landon was able to defeat pro-British voices in Washington that wanted to defer to Britain's eagerness to dominate postwar Thailand. Landon was also sympathetic to the Vietnamese nationalists in their war against the French. After a weeklong meeting with Ho Chi Minh early in 1946, Landon wrote what later became the document of earliest date in the Pentagon Papers.

Landon's wife, fellow missionary Margaret Landon, portrayed the Thai people sympathetically in her book of 1944, presented as a true story but actually a work of fiction, *Anna and the King of Siam*.[17] The novel was the basis for several Hollywood movies and the Rodgers and Hammerstein stage classic *The King and I*. Later critics correctly pointed to patronizing, Orientalist aspects of this romantic tale. But this former Presbyterian missionary created the most enduring popular image of an Asian national group, and one in which the local leader, the Thai king, invited respect by maintaining his country's independence from colonial powers.

Throughout the Cold War missionary-connected lobbyists and government officials were, with some exceptions, more tolerant of the anti-American postures of postcolonial regimes than were the policy makers they tried to influence in the administrations of Truman, Eisenhower, Kennedy, and Johnson. Missionary cosmopolitans tried to persuade these officials that the interests of the United States were consistent with the self-declared interest of decolonizing peoples. They lost the argument concerning China, the Arab world, and, most significantly, Vietnam. But missionary service programs did greatly influence

US-backed development programs in Asia, Africa, and Latin America, and eventually served as the explicit model for the Peace Corps.

In academia, missionary cosmopolitanism had its most dramatic and sweeping postwar impact. Long before Edward Said's *Orientalism*, the highly effective polemic of 1978 that named and criticized Western habits of derogatory thought about the peoples and cultures of the East, missionary-connected American professors had been pushing against many of the same biases. They led the postwar expansion of scholarship and teaching about recent and contemporary non-Western societies and cultures. Half of the presidents of the Association for Asian Studies during the two decades after the war were former missionaries or missionary children. The most influential was Edwin Reischauer, a historian who, along with his colleague John K. Fairbank, developed an East Asian Studies program at Harvard University that produced dozens of doctoral alumni who then launched comparable programs in universities and colleges throughout the United States. Reischauer also served as the American ambassador to Japan, the country of his birth.

Missionaries and their children were uniquely qualified for academic jobs because of their mastery of Asian languages and their familiarity with Asian cultures. Missionary son W. Norman Brown played in South Asian Studies a role comparable to Reischauer's in Japanese Studies. Political scientists Lucian Pye and A. Doak Barnett, literary scholar Harriet Mills, and historians C. Martin Wilbur, L. Carrington Goodrich, and Kenneth Scott Latourette increased the size and enhanced the reputation of Chinese Studies programs at Columbia, Yale, Michigan, and other universities. Although the Jewish Americans who joined faculties in large numbers at the same historical moment usually specialized in other, Eurocentric fields, campuses were major sites where missionary cosmopolitanism and Jewish cosmopolitanism operated simultaneously with a high level of intensity.

All of these examples of missionary cosmopolitanism involve Asia and the Middle East, not Africa and Latin America. Why that imbalance? The long-term diplomatic and commercial engagement of the United States with Latin America rendered public and private authorities less dependent on missionary expertise. In addition, Spanish was a familiar language, widely taught in American schools. And because ecumenical Protestants were often reluctant to "poach" on the strong Catholic presence in Latin America, the missionary presence there was dominated by evangelicals much less deferential to Catholics and even less likely to have important careers in secular institutions. Finally, Latin America was not a major theater in World War II, with the result that the US government did not have a great need to draw on Latin American expertise. Africa, too, was marginal to the war. African peoples spoke many different languages, none of which had the broad currency of Arabic, Chinese, Japanese, and several other Asian languages. Also, many societies in Asia and the Middle East were connected to ancient, classical cultures whose value was more quickly recognized in the North Atlantic West than the indigenous cultures of Africa and Latin America. Although there were missionaries to the Pacific islands, they were relatively few in number and learned languages of limited strategic value.

Within the churches, the missionary witness to the scope of humankind and the integrity of its many cultures threatened the old habit of speaking of non-Christians as "heathens." Some missionaries did persist in describing Muslims, Hindus, and adherents of other faiths in this manner, thereby reinforcing the traditions of white supremacy. But by the 1920s this outlook was on the defensive in church publications and in denominational assemblies.

Two missionaries with extensive experience in the field led the assault on the white supremacy of traditional missionary theory and practice. Daniel J. Fleming argued that "God has not been working exclusively through Christianity." From his post at Union Theological Seminary, where he taught for three decades after returning from service in India, Fleming ridiculed missionary arrogance and American complacency. He invited readers of the *Christian Century* to ask themselves how they would feel if a group of Buddhists came to their home town in Connecticut or Indiana and demanded that they give up Christianity and become Buddhists.[18] E. Stanley Jones declared Gandhi to be "one of the most Christlike men in history."[19] This Hindu had done more than thousands of missionary preachers like himself, Jones insisted, to show the world what true Christianity actually was. Jones was moved when Dana Tagore, the brother of the great poet and philosopher Rabindranath Tagore, told him that the Americans he had met bore little resemblance to the Jesus that the Tagore brothers had read about in the Bible. *Time* magazine followed Jones's activities and in 1929 reported that his book of 1925, *The Christ of the Indian Road*, had been translated into fourteen languages. Fleming and Jones hoped India would eventually turn to the Christian faith, but the chastening message to churchgoers in America was clear. If even an entirely foreign religion like Hinduism could be a stage on the way to heaven, surely the Christian faith must be understood as commodious. Its many versions should be tolerated rather than fraught by sectarian disputes. Ecumenical attitudes were essential to the survival of the faith in a diverse world filled with cultures that were not going to disappear.

Fleming pled with his fellow Christians to attend conscien-
tiously to "comparative studies in religion," an enterprise being
carried out with increasing determination in American seminaries and universities. Scholars who had been missionaries themselves or who relied heavily on missionary testimony had developed this field of study by the time of the Chicago World's Fair
in 1893, where the World's Parliament of Religions called popular
attention to it. Later generations were rightly sensitive to the
ways in which these scholars classified as "religions" on a Judeo-
Christian model a number of exceedingly diverse cultural projects. But the impact at the time was to vastly expand the capacity
of American and European Christians to achieve a measure of
empathic identification with an imposing range of cultures.

Faiths long scorned for "bowing down to wood and stone,"
as in the popular hymn "From Greenland's Icy Mountains,"
turned out to be highly complex, deeply grounded, sensitive
responses to the experience of human beings in a variety of historical contexts, and to share important features with Christianity itself. The popular dissemination of "The World's Great Religions" throughout much of the twentieth century was largely
the work of former missionaries. Japan-born Edmund D. Soper's textbook, *The Religions of Mankind*, was first published in
1921 and went through several editions.[20]

The tide of empathic identification with non-Christian
peoples was so strong by the early 1930s that it generated a comprehensive review of the entire missionary endeavor. The ecumenical reformers succeeded in persuading John D. Rockefeller
Jr. to fund a nine-month inquiry in which fifteen church leaders
toured the mission fields of India, Burma, China, and Japan. The
group was to prepare a comprehensive assessment of the missionary enterprise and chart a viable future for it. Rockefeller

bought the idea and capitalized the entire undertaking. The result was *Re-Thinking Missions: A Laymen's Inquiry after One Hundred Years*, a 1932 volume timed for the centennial of the beginning of American Protestant foreign missions.[21]

This volume became the foundational document for missionary cosmopolitanism's campaign to revolutionize American Protestant missions. *Re-Thinking Missions* was edited and largely written by Harvard philosopher William Ernest Hocking, best known for his *Meaning of God in Human Experience* (1912).[22] Hocking was also known for a critique of American cultural arrogance that matched that of Margaret Mead, Ruth Benedict, and other cultural anthropologists of the era. By what right, Hocking asked, "do we apply our standards of civilization to cultures other than our own?"[23]

Re-Thinking Missions, otherwise known as the Hocking Report, declared that what really mattered about missions was not preaching but "educational and other philanthropic" activities. Trying to persuade people to give up their own religion to become Christians was no longer a good idea. "We must be willing" to provide services to Indigenous people in need, the report insisted, "without any preaching." We must "cooperate with non-Christian agencies for social improvement," a crucial portion of the text continued, and we must respond to "the initiative of the Orient in defining the ways in which we shall be invited to help." The missionary should be "a learner and a coworker," not a preacher. The task of evangelism, in this view, was to be done by exemplifying "the Christian way of life and its spirit" and "by quiet personal contact and by contagion." Any evangelizing done at all was to be done "not by word but by deed" and, as the report emphasized in its own italics, "*by living and by human service.*" There was no dodging the responsibility to engage the social evils found in many societies. "Missions should recognize and teach that a well ordered community cannot exist when there are too great inequalities," the report proclaimed. In a characteristic equivocation when it came to actual politics, Hocking and his colleagues explained that they were not advocating "meddling in politics," especially those of foreign countries, yet Christians "can wisely attempt to modify any social order which unduly accentuates economic inequality and privilege." Pushing the social reform envelope as far as its authors thought they could, *Re-Thinking Missions* allowed that "if one man by the honest study of Christ's teaching becomes a communist, another a labor union leader, another a socialist and another a capitalist, none should find himself excluded from the fellowship or prevented from trying to win other Christians to his point of view."[24]

Communism potentially compatible with Christianity? Shocking enough, but that was far from the end of it. The top Methodist missionary in India, Bishop Frederick Bohn Fisher, told readers of the *Christian Century* that the Hocking Report, which went through ten printings in six months, was "a book of human rights with a bomb in every chapter."[25] No bomb was bigger than the report's perspective on the religions practiced in the East. These faiths were not such terrible things, according to Hocking and his colleagues. While Christianity could be expected to emerge eventually as the faith of all humankind, for the time being Christians should respect and in some cases even support other religions. It may well be that Christ's ultimate triumph will be advanced by "the immediate strengthening of several of the present religions of Asia." The big problem in the world in 1932 was not the power of other religions, as had so often been assumed, but secularism: missions need to be mobilized in an alliance of all religions against "the same menace, the spread of the secular spirit." In a characteristically generous gesture toward Hinduism, the report described child marriage as an abuse that had "invaded" that religion. When missionaries criticized such abuses, they should see themselves as "joining Hindus" in clarifying and purifying their own faith. "Desiring to be considered a co-worker rather than an enemy," the ideal Christian will "refrain from misrepresentation abroad of the evils he desires to cure" and will make a point of calling attention to "the efforts being made by nationals to correct" those evils.[26]

Stop preaching the gospel to the Hindus and Muslims and Buddhists? Acknowledge the spark of divinity within those religions? The evangelical wing of Protestantism would have nothing to do with such ideas. Evangelicals held firm to the notion that the unconverted were forever lost and that converts were expected to follow American models for what it meant to be a good Christian. Conservatives continued to treat the Bible as the unchanging, inerrant word of God, no matter what the historical context in which this or that bit of scripture had been created. In missionary theory, Protestantism's two-party system was fully in operation.

At the time of its publication, Re-Thinking Missions was too radical even for a great many on the ecumenical side of the ecumenical-evangelical divide. Yet from the mid-1930s through the 1960s the major denominations gradually reformed their missionary activities in accord with the once-controversial document's prescriptions. The Hocking Report was rarely cited to justify these changes—it was a "red flag"—but the ideas it brought together and popularized were increasingly accepted by missionary boards and by newly recruited missionary personnel associated with the so-called mainline American Protestant denominations. "Foreign" missions became "the world mission," and converts in several mission fields were given more and more authority over operations.

As concerns about "cultural imperialism" intensified, the number of American missionaries sent abroad by the Congregationalists, Presbyterians, Methodists, Northern Baptists, Dutch Reformed, and other ecumenically dominated denominations decreased. The Hocking Report assumed the missionary project would flourish, but on revised terms. It did so only temporarily. The service-centered approach urged by the Hocking Report was eventually separated from the very concept of missions. The "Global Christianity" that replaced "missions" in the "mainline" denominations placed great emphasis on the agency of indigenous peoples. By the late 1960s, the majority of Americans abroad who called themselves "missionaries" were sponsored by the Southern Baptists, the Christian Missionary Alliance, the Seventh-day Adventists, the Assemblies of God, and other evangelical denominations and agencies.

Prior to this shift of missionary energy from the ecumenical to the evangelical camp, the ecumenicals began to sharply question the importance of denominational distinctions. Meaningful as the distinction between a Northern and Southern Presbyterian might be to the faithful in Maryland or Kentucky, it made no sense abroad. To join the Dutch Reformed or the Disciples of Christ, what did it matter? Seeing the home churches through the eyes of converts in Korea or Lebanon or Nigeria revealed the parochialism of American Protestant denominations. Perhaps it was time that Western Christians joined forces institutionally? The Christian project, for all its versions, was understood to be a single, if commodious, enterprise. Denominations were mere historical instantiations. Was it time to get beyond them?

While the ecumenical intelligentsia was pondering this question, its members read a commanding piece of historical sociology that appeared in 1929, *The Social Sources of Denominationalism*. This book, by Yale University's H. Richard Niebuhr (Reinhold

Niebuhr's brother) explained the historical conditions that had fragmented the gospel. Denominationalism was an evil to be overcome. Niebuhr's critique of denominationalism was inspired by German scholarship and betrayed very little missionary influence. But Niebuhr offered irrefutable evidence that Christians had repeatedly fashioned the gospel in highly particular ways, as responses to local conditions. His theologically sensitive analysis spoke exactly to the concerns of the missionary cosmopolitans. "A church is needed which has transcended the divisions of the world and has adjusted itself not to the local interests and needs of classes, races, or nations, but to the common interests of mankind and to the constitution of the unrealized kingdom of God. No denominational Christianity, no matter how broad its scope, suffices for this task. The church which proclaim this gospel must be one in which no national allegiance will be suffered to infringe on the unity of an international fellowship."[27] Why not establish a single, national Protestant church? Well before Niebuhr's ambitious treatise, YMCA leader Sherwood Eddy asked readers of the *Christian Century* in 1920 to consider the possibility that the churches in the mission field might instruct those at home.[28]

The momentum for mergers gathered in the United States year by year. Union Theological Seminary president Henry P. Van Dusen declared in 1947 that the example of a single, national Christian church in India could serve as a model for Christians in the United States. Perhaps, mused Van Dusen, denominational distinctions within the North Atlantic West, including America, would be overcome at last? Perhaps the "receiving" churches created by foreign missions could become a model for the "sending" churches?[29]

Ecumenical leaders deliberated about this while they tried to act more comprehensively on their growing historical sophistication, their increasingly resolute globalism, and their accelerating recognition of the diversity of American society. They tried to develop a version of Christianity suitable for their own time and place, yet consistent with a single, universally applicable gospel.

What might that gospel be? How might Christianity look if it were true to its deepest values yet functional in a demographically diverse, sexually and racially egalitarian, globally engaged, and scientifically literate society welcoming to Jews and to other non-Christians? And a society that was, moreover, experiencing rapid urbanization, the expansion of education at all levels, and greater immersion in world affairs?

Church officials, seminary professors, and preachers recognized only gradually the severity of this challenge and the many domains in which it demanded attention. How they tried to meet this cascading challenge, and how their more conservative Protestant contemporaries reacted to their initiatives, is the central dynamic in Christianity's relation to the public affairs of the United States during the past one hundred years.

5

The Apotheosis of Liberal Protestantism

Am I a soldier of the cross? . . .
Must I be carried to the skies
On flow'ry beds of ease,
While others fought to win the prize,
And sailed through bloody seas? . . .
Must I not stem the flood?

—ISAAC WATTS, 1721

AMERICANS ARE not "a Christian people" and should stop describing themselves that way, insisted Union Seminary theologian and political theorist John C. Bennett in 1958. In *Christians and the State*, Bennett explained to his own Protestant tribe that T. S. Eliot's widely admired *The Idea of a Christian Society* could not apply to the United States. The American government was properly understood as a secular instrument. American society and its civic instruments were religiously pluralistic.

Jews and missionaries were helping the nation to understand its own true character. Bennett knew that Jews were not the only diversifiers, but he was explicit about their centrality. He said that the entirety of *Christians and the State*—a book that reflected the progressive opinions of the ecumenical intelligentsia of the late 1950s—was informed by "the contributions of the Jewish people to the common morality." Jews were a reminder of the necessity for a pluralistic perspective, but they were more than that. Jews "have often been more sensitive than Christians to the problems of justice." Jews could help Christians recognize their own calling to make the world a better place. Missionaries, too, helped American Christians recognize this, and to understand the limits of their own sectarianism and ethnocentrism. "The missionary movement," Bennett wrote, is an "astonishing example of the capacity of Christians to identify themselves with people in other nations." In keeping with the boomerang effect, missionaries often become "so identified with the nations to which they go that they represent them to the nations from which they come."[1]

Bennett was surrounded by well-positioned defenders of the idea of a "Christian nation." Only a few years before, in 1949, the National Association of Evangelicals, the largest transdenominational organization of conservative Christians, had proposed an amendment to the Constitution: "This nation devoutly recognizes the authority and law of Jesus Christ, Savior and Ruler of nations, through whom we are bestowed the blessings of Almighty God." Then in 1954 Republican senator Ralph Flanders of Vermont proposed a similar amendment, inserting God and Jesus into the Constitution. Neither effort prevailed, partly because ecumenical leaders like Bennett allied themselves with the forty-one Jewish organizations that formally registered their opposition to the "Flanders Amendment."[2]

These mid-twentieth-century victories by the ecumenical leaders over their evangelical rivals were brief moments in a multidecade campaign to achieve a more cosmopolitan Protestantism. This campaign developed by fits and starts as its leaders responded to and participated in a succession of political and cultural movements in the society at large. What most defined the campaign was a series of demands it made, one after another, on American Protestants. The liberalizers called on the faithful to renounce a number of inherited ideas and practices the ecumenical elite decided were racist, sexist, imperialist, homophobic, unscientific, and chauvinistic, and thus inconsistent with the gospel as it should apply to modern American society.

But these ideas and practices remained popular with much of the white population, within and beyond the churches. How far could the leadership go without losing the people in the pews? How little change would suffice to remain true to the gospel as the ecumenical elite were coming to understand it?

The campaign had strong support from many congregations, but it was largely a top-down operation. A globally conscious ecclesiastical intelligentsia sought to inspire churchgoers to discard anachronisms and to embrace a gospel whose timelessness was proven by its ability to adapt to changing conditions. The campaign was never a single, tightly organized enterprise with a fixed agenda; rather, it was a series of loosely connected initiatives advanced through the Federal Council of Churches, the National Council of Churches, the World Council of Churches, Church Women United, the YMCA, the YWCA, and the social justice committees of several major denominations, especially the Congregationalists and the Methodists. In contrast to the "Christian nationalism" favored by evangelicals, the ecumenicals led a movement that a number of historians have recently come to call "Christian globalism."[3]

The campaign went through several chronologically distinct phases. It achieved its greatest influence on public affairs during the 1940s. Conservative opposition in the early and mid-1950s forced it to be more cautious. The campaign rebounded in the early 1960s and intensified when ecumenical leaders, in an unprecedented episode in collective self-criticism, demanded more of their churchgoers than ever before. Later in that decade, ecumenical denominations began to lose members just as their officers took bolder stands on the political issues of the day, especially civil rights and the Vietnam War. By the end of the twentieth century, leaders of the campaign were confronted with an altogether unexpected and deeply distressing reality: the evangelicals had grown in numbers and public influence while ecumenical churches had lost about a third of their members. In this last phase, which continues into the third decade of the twenty-first century, ecumenical leaders were inclined to think of their churches as a "prophetic minority," bearing progressive witness against an alliance of evangelicals and conservative, antistatist political forces.

In the early 1920s the ecumenical campaign for a more cosmopolitan Protestantism got going, building on the Social Gospel that had flourished during the Progressive Era.[4] The liberalizers, often called "modernists" in this early period, prioritized what they saw as Christian responsibilities in the world. Individual salvation was important, but more pressing was the duty to make the world a better place. "I will show you my faith by my works," wrote the biblical James.[5] The modernists were not troubled by evolution, and they engaged modern science sympathetically. They welcomed scholarly discoveries about the historical origins of the books of the Bible. Many of them continued to endorse Wilsonian visions of world order even in the face of popular isolationism.

Opposing these relatively cosmopolitan views—and defined in large part by reaction against them—were the fundamentalists.

In historian George M. Marsden's classic formulation, the Fundamentalist movement was a "federation of co-belligerents united by their fierce opposition to modernist attempts to bring Christianity into line with modern thought."[6]

But the fundamentalists were innovators of their own kind. What they often claimed was a stable orthodoxy was in fact only a particular slice of the Protestant tradition. The notion that the Bible was "inerrant," for example, was not central to the teachings of either of the two Protestant families in the nineteenth century and did not gain much traction among theological conservatives until very late in that century. The ferocity with which early twentieth-century fundamentalists asserted the inerrancy doctrine was quite novel. The fundamentalists also had an innovative theory of history, according to which an elaborate series of divine "dispensations" led to the apocalypse and the eventual reign of Christ. Moreover, the fundamentalists developed the evangelical family's individualist theme in tune with the free-market ideology of modern business corporations.[7]

The liberalizers made extensive use of the Federal Council of Churches, founded in 1908 as a Social Gospel coalition of denominational bodies that previously had lacked a means of acting together. While overwhelmingly a white organization, the FCC by the early 1920s included the four largest African American denominations among its affiliates: the African Methodist Episcopal Church, the African American Episcopal Zion Church, the Colored Methodist Episcopal Church, and the National Baptist Convention. The missionary-saturated FCC opposed immigration restrictions and hired a full-time organizer— former missionary Sidney Gulick—to lobby against them.[8] This liberal immigration policy typified the ecumenical elite's willingness to get well out in front of the people in the pews. Many rural and small-town churchgoers affiliated with FCC-affiliated denominations joined their fundamentalist neighbors in swelling the size of the nativist and racist rallies of the Ku Klux Klan during the 1920s.[9]

The campaign for a more cosmopolitan Protestantism was visible in almost every issue of two prominent magazines, *World Tomorrow* and *Christian Century*. It was in vogue at several leading schools of divinity, most conspicuously Union Theological Seminary in New York. Union's Reinhold Niebuhr cemented his reputation in 1932 with *Moral Man and Immoral Society*, a book urging Christians to recognize that violence on the part of oppressed workers might well be necessary.[10] Further to the left, Union's Harry F. Ward was credited with—and blamed for—inspiring students to raise a red flag over the seminary on May Day 1934. Ward served for twenty years as chairman of the American Civil Liberties Union. Congregationalists and Methodists took the lead against Jim Crow and economic inequality at home and against colonialism abroad. The dean of Methodist-sponsored Duke Divinity School warned a convention of Methodists in 1926 that Americans had no business telling people in foreign lands about their moral failings so long as the United States tolerated racial segregation.[11] Elsewhere, activist clergy decried inhumane working conditions in mines and factories. The National Conference of Christians and Jews promoted the full acceptance of Jews into American life and opposed the urban missions designed to convert immigrant Jews to Christianity.

During these interwar years, Protestantism's two-party system was on full display but did not map exactly onto denominational distinctions, nor was it coterminal with the two-party system of electoral politics. Throughout the 1920s, most ecumenical Protestants outside the Democrats' "Solid South" were comfortable with the relatively conservative Republican Party.

Democrat Franklin Roosevelt eventually did win the support of many of these northern, midwestern, and western ecumenicals, especially after he became president, but Republican loyalty remained strong. The Republican tilt of these ecumenical Protestants should not be confused with support for the more sweeping antistate ideologies embraced by the loudest voices in the evangelical camp.[12] As the ecumenical-evangelical divide sharpened, it tracked long-term conflicts between narrowly individual and more broadly social narratives of salvation. Simply declaring one's "belief in Christ" appeared to be enough for many Christians who could then celebrate money making and free enterprise with a clear conscience.[13] For others, what mattered was applying the lessons of the parable of the Good Samaritan.[14]

In the 1940s Samaritan-inspired ecumenical leaders of both political parties gave particular attention to the evils of racism, anti-Semitism, nationalism, colonialism, and economic inequality. Individuals with missionary connections wrote the campaign's most influential theoretical treatises, staffed its major transdenominational organizations, and supervised its most important conferences. The FCC convened several wartime conventions that brought hundreds of church leaders together, demanding economic justice in the United States and, in some instances, even asking for a reconsideration of the whole notion of private ownership. These conferences were organized by the FCC's Commission for a Just and Durable Peace, chaired by John Foster Dulles, who was then known primarily as a Presbyterian layman.[15] The voting delegates in these gatherings called for the liberation of colonized peoples, a category in which they included Puerto Ricans along with the inhabitants of Japanese-occupied Korea. The Dulles Commission encouraged the creation of institutions capable of defending human rights globally and expressed sympathy even for the notion of what was frankly called "world government." *Time* magazine described the leftward tilt of the FCC as "sensational."[16]

The Roosevelt administration encouraged and supported the FCC's work during the war years. The State Department invited the Dulles Commission's March 1942 conference to discuss a draft of what became one of Roosevelt's most celebrated speeches, his radical 1944 State of the Union address proposing an "economic bill of rights." Federal authorities authorized exceptions to wartime restrictions on travel to enable the FCC to bring its forces together to advance progressive agendas. Roosevelt's team solicited the FCC as an ally in creating the United Nations and welcomed its influence in drafting the UN Charter.

At the San Francisco meeting founding the UN in 1945, the campaign for a more cosmopolitan Protestantism made its most striking and enduring mark on the history of the era. The FCC group argued successfully for a Commission on Human Rights and for a Trusteeship Council charged with facilitating the movement of colonized peoples to independence. The ecumenical lobby also defeated an effort by the British delegation to guarantee the right to proselytize, which the American group opposed on the grounds that it would insult Jews, Muslims, Buddhists, and other non-Christians. Despite elements of patronizing paternalism, the anticolonialism and antiracism of the ecumenical leadership was far from routine for the time. Saturated with former missionaries and other missionary-connected Americans, and working in close cooperation with lobbyists from the American Jewish Committee, the FCC so substantially influenced the UN Charter that, in the words of historian Samuel Moyn, its leaders "were by any standard most responsible for the original move to the internationalization of religious freedom and, in fact, for the presence of the entire notion of human rights in international affairs."[17] The FCC "issued its own list of human rights," historian Gene Zubovich observes, "encompassing virtually every demand of the African American political struggle of the era."[18]

The ecumenical intelligentsia at this 1940s high point took for granted that Protestant Christianity was the proper foundation for world order and that it was up to Americans to establish it. Although these ecumenical leaders worked closely with Jewish groups, they had no doubt that their authority derived from their position as the authentic spokespersons for global Christianity. They were highly suspicious of Catholics, whose record on human rights in Europe fueled their contempt. They paid no attention to fundamentalist constructions of the faith then being proclaimed with new fervor by the National Association of Evangelicals.

Throughout the 1940s, these liberalizers continued to speak casually of the United States as "a Christian nation." Only gradually did the ecumenical elite come around to renouncing this characterization, first through an embrace of the intermediate notion of a Judeo-Christian America and then, by the 1960s, dispensing with it altogether. The FCC leaders also assumed that it was no great challenge to identify just what were the truly Christian principles. Now and then, someone spelled out those principles. Lutheran official Frederick Nolde, the leader of the FCC group at the San Francisco meeting of the UN, proclaimed their liberal universalism in 1946: "The Christian gospel relates to all men, regardless of race, language, or color. . . . There is no Christian basis to support a fancied intrinsic superiority of any one race. . . . The rights and freedoms of all peoples in all lands should be recognized and safeguarded. Freedom of religion and religious worship, of speech, of assembly, of the press, of cultural interchange, of scientific inquiry and teaching are fundamental to human development and in keeping with the moral law. International cooperation is needed to create conditions under which these freedoms become a reality."[19]

At this 1940s moment, the FCC represented more than thirty denominations. It was by far the largest predominantly white organization in the United States to demand an end to racial segregation as early as 1946, declaring it to be "a violation of the Gospel of love and human brotherhood."[20] At a time when nearly all national organizations, including the National Association of Evangelicals, were willing to hold conventions in cities whose hotels would not accommodate African Americans, the FCC repeatedly scheduled its meetings in Philadelphia and Cleveland, two cities whose hotel associations promised that African American delegates would not be refused service.

In 1946, too, the Congregationalists called for an end to Jim Crow throughout the country, and both the YMCA and the YWCA integrated their national organizations. Many local congregations and Y offices in the southern states resisted the integrationist initiatives of the national leadership. But the FCC encouraged its southern affiliates to work toward "a nonsegregated society" as well as "a non-segregated church." Local congregations in every region of the country remained overwhelming white or Black. A handful of Black religious leaders became regulars on FCC committees and commissions, including George C. Haynes, C. E. Tobias, Howard Thurman, and especially Benjamin Mays, who in 1944 was elected an FCC vice president.[21] Beyond the FCC, a radical fringe of ecumenical activists associated with the Fellowship of Reconciliation, led by missionary son George Houser and African American activist Bayard Rustin, carried out the first "freedom ride" in 1947, challenging segregated public accommodations in Virginia and North Carolina.[22]

Newly organized churchwomen added heft to the campaign for a more cosmopolitan Protestantism. Women from throughout ecumenical Protestantism joined together in 1941 to form what was eventually called Church Women United. The immediate impetus was the ostensibly egalitarian decision of one denomination after another in the 1930s to abolish separate women's missionary boards, traditionally the largest women's organizations in American Protestantism. But men overwhelmingly dominated the comprehensive boards and commissions into which the women's groups were folded. Irritated by this manifest demotion under the guise of integration, activist women from several major denominations established a transdenominational organization that claimed from its start to represent ten million women from seventy denominations. It accepted into membership any women, including African Americans, who shared their goals even if they were not members of any church.

Church Women United was consistently more liberal than the FCC itself and most of the denominational governing bodies. These women generally shared with their husbands a loyalty to the liberal wing of the Republican Party, but "they prided themselves," notes one historian, "on taking positions and making public pronouncements with little regard" for what the male-dominated "officialdom" might say.[23] They were "Christians," of course, but their focus was institutional rather than doctrinal. Their most important identity was as "churchwomen." They were less inclined than their male counterparts to cite scripture. While they pressed for more authority in governance, they usually downplayed the ordination of women because they understood it as a trap, whereby women would be obliged to conform to a decidedly male frame for leadership. Some feared that men would leave the churches if they lost their monopoly on the pulpit. But as soon as they organized themselves, the church-women became formidable players in the campaign for a more cosmopolitan Protestantism. Church Women United was "often in the vanguard," observes historian Martin E. Marty, "on issues of world affairs, civil rights, human rights, employed women . . . and ecumenism."[24]

Antiracist treatises written by two male seminary professors further illustrate the nature of the liberalizers campaign during the 1940s. *Color and Conscience: The Irrepressible Conflict* (1946), by Congregationalist Buell G. Gallagher of the Pacific School of Religion in Berkeley, California, was a systematic distillation of lessons American Protestants had learned through the foreign missionary project. Gallagher complained that "the Christian Church" had failed to produce "an ethical attack" on racism nearly as strong as that produced by the Communist Party. At Garrett Theological Seminary in Evanston, Illinois, Methodist Edmund D. Soper, a Japan-born missionary son, published *Racism: A World Issue* (1947). Like Gallagher, Soper attacked anti-Semitism as well as anti-Black racism and other kinds of prejudice against communities of descent. Both writers treated racism within the United States as a national instantiation of worldwide white supremacy. Here, as in the wartime conferences of the FCC, domestic antiracism and Christian globalism reinforced each other.[25]

The writings of intellectuals like Soper and Gallagher did not reflect the opinions of the average churchgoer, even within the Congregationalists, Methodists, Episcopalians, and other liberal denominations. But the relative indifference the liberalizers often encountered in their own churches was nothing compared to the open and volatile opposition they faced from their evangelical rivals. Representatives of the National Association of Evangelicals asked the State Department to reject the UN's

Declaration of Human Rights because its inclusion of social and economic rights was "socialistic." The United Nations itself, in which the ecumenicals had so much invested, troubled evangelicals because it lacked an avowed biblical foundation. Some evangelicals described the World Council of Churches, founded in Amsterdam in 1948 but dominated by American ecumenical leaders, as an instrument of Satan. Evangelicals routinely accused officers of the WCC and the National Council of Churches of communist sympathies and even of Communist Party affiliations, charges that increased in frequency and volume during the period of the Red Scare from the late 1940s through the 1950s.

One McCarthy Era episode had especially far-ranging consequences for the balance of power between ecumenical and evangelical Protestants. This was oil magnate J. Howard Pew's shift of financial support from the former to the latter. In 1950, when the FCC was in the process of reconstituting itself as the National Council of Churches and bringing in a number of new affiliate denominations, Pew organized the National Lay Committee, a group of eighty-five politically conservative Presbyterian and Episcopalian laymen determined to ensure that the newly powerful National Council did not promote the federal regulation of American business. Pew hosted retreats and conferences for conservative churchmen and corporate leaders. When the NCC issued "Basic Christian Principles and Assumptions for Economic Life," reflecting a broadly social democratic outlook, Pew's committee repudiated it as "socialist" and demanded that the NCC honor the American "free enterprise" system for its contributions to "human welfare, to the establishment of freedom, justice, and order and in the implementation of Christian principles." The quarrel simmered along for several years until 1955, when a new NCC president, Presbyterian

Eugene Carson Blake, wrote Pew a letter highly critical of the activities of the Lay Committee. Pew then left the NCC and took his money and his wealthy supporters to the evangelicals, immediately funding the new magazine, *Christianity Today*. Central to the imbroglio was the demand of Pew and his allies for "a more militant voice in the Cold War, consistent defense of laissez-faire free enterprise economics as the sole Christian pattern, and theological conservatism."[26]

Yet even in the restrained atmosphere of the 1950s, when Pew's departure cut the campaign's financial resources, transdenominational youth organizations engaged in activities that were far to the left. The Student Volunteer Movement, which had originated as a major recruiter of missionaries but had become an all-purpose youth organization, brought thousands of Black and white college students together in a series of weeklong conferences led by Methodist and Presbyterian women with missionary experience. Attendees of these Christian globalist and antiracist events, held on university campuses in Ohio, included three groups of young people otherwise largely isolated from one another: foreign students from Africa and Asia then studying in the United States, Black students from Morehouse, Fisk, and other African American colleges, and white students from leading universities and liberal arts colleges. Until then, hardly any of the white attendees had ever experienced personal contact with their Black contemporaries.

One historian describes these multiracial events as "a subversive thread within mainline Protestantism," recruiting at the height of the Cold War a generation of students who in the following decade participated in Freedom Rides and other kinds of civil rights activism.[27] Several of these conferences asked attendees to be prepared to discuss the anti-imperialist book *Encounter with Revolution* (1955), by the radical Presbyterian missionary to Latin America M. Richard Shaull.[28] Later recognized as a precursor of Liberation Theology, this book insisted that religion and politics could not be separated and that it was the duty of Christians to join indigenous revolutionary movements.

John C. Bennett was not as extreme as Shaull, but his *Christians and the State* invites further attention as a revealing window on how the ecumenical leaders at the end of the 1950s felt about themselves and about the United States. The NCC had enjoyed a few years to catch its political and financial breath following Pew's epic departure. Bennett called upon "the ecumenical Christian community," as he referred to his own tribe, to perfect its witness in domestic and international political arenas. He welcomed Jewish allies, religious or secular, as well as "atheists or agnostics or Naturalistic Humanists," as citizens of equal standing. Bennett urged Christians to listen to the criticisms of traditional religion voiced by nonbelievers. We should "recognize without the least condescension" that these secular intellectuals offer criticisms of traditional religion that "are often valid." The atheists, Bennett explained, "represent a challenge to obscurantism and clericalism that is needed." Religious people tend toward "stuffiness" if they "never have to face this kind of opposition."[29] Throughout *Christians and the State*, Bennett remained confident that ecumenical Protestantism was strong enough to survive any challenge. Even atheists could be welcomed into the conversation.

In offering a collegial hand to atheists, Bennett was pushing against a well-established ecumenical as well as evangelical habit of railing against "secularism." Ecumenical leaders raised relatively few objections in 1954 when Congress added "under God" to the Pledge of Allegiance. Writing God into the Constitution was too much, but putting him in the pledge was a step they could tolerate even if was not consistent with their cosmopolitan aspirations. Eisenhower's endlessly quoted asser-tion that "our form of government has no sense unless it is founded in a deeply felt religious faith, and I don't care what it is" dates from this era.[30] References to the deity in the pledge and, after 1956, in the official national motto, "In God We Trust," were only a minor annoyance for Bennett and his colleagues as long as they were in charge of what "God" meant.

And they did expect to remain in charge. They had the fran-chise. They approached the 1960s with high hopes about the capacity of the nation to respond to their ongoing campaign. Since the evangelicals soon eclipsed them in the national arena, one can wonder what made people like Bennett so sure of them-selves. Several historic conditions inspired this confidence.

Church membership in the ecumenical denominations was at an all-time high by the late 1950s, reversing a decline experi-enced during the interwar years. Many of the new Presbyteri-ans, Lutherans, and Methodists in the growing suburbs were upwardly mobile whites who left the Church of the Nazarene or the Seventh-day Adventists to join recognizably middle-class congregations. Yet a demographic fact rarely noticed at the time was that increases in ecumenical membership barely kept pace with the growth of the national population. Even in the great "joining" years of the 1950s, no more than one-third of the na-tional population ever became formally affiliated with "main-line" denominations, even though two-thirds identified with them when polled by social scientists and journalists. Individu-als with at least a tribal connection to the mainline denomina-tions remained in charge of nearly all major public and private institutions. One way to join the establishment was to go to the right church, or to say that you did.

Bennett and his cohort had additional reasons to feel opti-mistic. By the end of the 1950s McCarthyism had been defeated.

The NCC celebrated in 1958 by calling for the diplomatic recognition of the People's Republic of China. The NCC was by far the largest American organization to do so by that time. *Time* paid close attention to the doings of the NCC and featured several of its leaders on its cover, including Blake and Henry Pitney Van Dusen. President Eisenhower, while always vague theologically, offered regular symbolic deference to churches, one of which—a Presbyterian congregation near the White House—he joined shortly after coming into office. Oxnam enjoyed regular, private correspondence with his old friend Dulles, then secretary of state, although Dulles consistently rejected Oxnam's counsel that the best way to defeat communism was not through military containment but through greater global economic equality. Further, the activities of Martin Luther King Jr. were a source of special pride for the ecumenical elite. King, who won national stature for his leadership of the Montgomery, Alabama, bus boycott and for his powerful preaching, was literally one of their own. He was trained at Boston University by L. Harold DeWolf, one of the most respected ecumenical theologians of the era. King's work in Alabama was a vital fulfilment of ecumenical appreciation for Gandhi's nonviolent approach to political change.

The ecumenical elite also took pride and comfort from the continued standing of Reinhold Niebuhr as a national sage. Niebuhr's reputation depended heavily upon his decades of espousing ideas that he defined as Christian but were consistent with the ethical self-conception of secular liberals. He credited Christianity with a series of insights necessary to a healthy democracy. He listed "a sense of awe before the vastness of the historical drama" of the times, "a sense of modesty" about the nation's capacities, "a sense of contrition about the common frailties" behind Soviet bravado and American vanity, and "a sense of gratitude for the divine mercies which are promised to those who humble themselves."[31] Secular critics complained that Niebuhr's "Christian realism" did not differ from the non-Christian realism of Cold War politics. But there were many "atheists for Niebuhr," as his secular admirers were sardonically called, because so many of his ideas could be accepted without having to "get religion." This was especially true of the insight Niebuhr is now most widely appreciated for proclaiming: that Americans too often approached world affairs with a dangerous innocence, failing to recognize America's own capacity for evil-doing.[32] Niebuhr gradually came around to agree with Bennett that it had been a mistake to keep calling the United States a "Christian nation" or even a "Judeo-Christian nation," but the great theologian coasted through the 1950s on the vague but wide-spread feeling that these still-popular ideas about American nationality were fully compatible with political liberalism.[33]

The high standing of another theologian, Paul Tillich, further contributed to the upbeat attitude with which most campaigners for a more cosmopolitan Protestantism rounded out the 1950s. The cultural narrowness of American Christians had been Tillich's bane since he immigrated from Germany in the 1930s, but now, at the height of his fame, he vowed more fiercely than ever to wage war "against any groups working for American provincialism." He pledged to help build "an America in which every provincialism, including theological and philosophical provincialism, is resisted and conquered."[34]

Operating in this confident manner, ecumenical leaders continued to regard white evangelicals as poor country cousins. Yet these alleged rustics, many of whom occupied urban pulpits and showed a media savvy well beyond that of most of their ecumenical peers, managed during the 1940s and 1950s to put in place an extensive institutional network that gradually gained more and more traction. Veteran preachers Harold Ockenga,

Carl F. H. Henry, and Charles Fuller tried to discard the widely discredited "fundamentalist" label and present their relatively unchanged movement to the world as "evangelical," appropriating for themselves a label that traditionally embraced a variety of nonfundamentalist orientations.

These enterprising captors of the old, honored label established their own transdenominational associations, schools, publishing houses, and radio and television networks. The National Association of Evangelicals was founded in 1942 as a lobbying organization and then proceeded to oppose one measure after another promoted by the Federal and National Councils of Churches. Fuller Theological Seminary, founded in 1947, became a concentrated intellectual force against the influence of the liberal seminaries. *Christianity Today* was founded in 1956 to counter the *Christian Century* and thanks to Pew, who financed the sending of free copies to thousands of Protestant clergy, immediately outpaced the *Century* in circulation. The old link between fundamentalist religion and antistatist politics was strengthened. Evangelicalism flourished not so much as the elongation of an old conservative theological tradition but as an aspect of social and economic modernization, closely tied to business and up-to-date methods of communication.

In two excellent books, historians Darren Dochuk and Kevin Kruse show how vital conservative oil money was to the rise of a religious right identifying antiregulation politics with Christianity.[35] *Christianity Today*, in its early years, encouraged its readers to regard racism as a sin to be cured not by the action of civil governments but by changes in the hearts of individuals. This magazine's editors debated among themselves what they should say about racial segregation and decided not to oppose it. The first article on the topic they published was indeed a defense of segregation.[36] Many evangelical magazines and radio programs disparaged the UN as insufficiently supportive of a Christian agenda, excoriated the NCC for its support of the recognition of "Red China," and depicted King's movement of African Americans as heavily influenced by communists. In 1959 *Christianity Today* editor Carl F. H. Henry declared that 105 ecumenical leaders had "Communist affiliations."[37] An expanding network of evangelical radio and television programs surrounded and eventually drowned out the radio sermons of the trademark ecumenical program, Ralph W. Sockman's National Radio Pulpit, broadcast by NBC Radio from 1928 to 1962. Although the full force of this evangelical apparatus was not felt until the 1970s and thereafter, even in the late 1950s it frustrated the ecumenical leadership's efforts to ignore it.

The ecumenical intelligentsia had an especially hard time ignoring Billy Graham, whose popularity soared in the 1950s. While building on the traditional population base of the fundamentalists, Graham reached out to Pentecostals. He was much less rigid, doctrinally, than most fundamentalist preachers, writers, and seminarians had been. He embraced more of contemporary popular culture than had the fundamentalists of old. He deliberately developed a celebrity image congruent with Hollywood conventions. Graham luxuriated in a personality that seemed garish to many "mainliners," and he often used undignified sales techniques, "pitching" the gospel to the public. He was "down to earth" in ways that most Presbyterian and Congregationalist ministers had been taught they should never be. Graham's style of religion amused and appalled seminary graduates proud of their learning in theology and biblical hermeneutics. Even as sympathetic a biographer as Grant Wacker finds "little evidence that Graham clearly understood" even the basics of the "higher criticism or related critical methods taught in the mainline seminaries."[38]

"The Bible says," Graham would proclaim, and what then might follow in Graham's sermons often amazed the seminary establishment, which generally agreed with Reinhold Niebuhr that Graham's religion lacked spiritual maturity and intellectual depth. Graham, wrote Niebuhr in *Life*, was unable to speak to anyone "aware of the continuing possibilities of good and evil in every advance of civilization, every discipline of culture, and every religious convention."[39] Graham was a prominent example of Niebuhr's trademark target, American innocence.

But Graham was most definitely changing the face of American Protestantism. His huge audiences were all the more relevant to the role of religion in American life when it became clear that they included an astonishing number of Presbyterians, Methodists, Disciples, and members of other ecumenically aligned denominations. Some mainline churchgoers were puzzled that their ministers were ambivalent about the charismatic preacher who brought real zing to religion, put it on the map of popular culture, and offered an easily accessible understanding of the Bible. Many of the millions drawn to Graham paid little attention to the political positions taken by the National Association of Evangelicals and by fundamentalist rabble-rousers like Carl McIntire but appreciated something Graham offered: a straightforward faith, apparently pure and simple.

Evangelical leaders further discredited themselves, in the eyes of the ecumenical intelligentsia, by opposing the election of a Catholic to the presidency in 1960. The National Association of Evangelicals warned that if John F. Kennedy were to be elected, "the United States will no longer be recognized as a Protestant nation in the eyes of the world."[40] The NAE did not formally endorse Richard M. Nixon's presidential candidacy, but its national office encouraged evangelical churches throughout the country to offer special election prayers on every

Sunday prior to the November election. Graham pretended to be neutral, but his friendship with Nixon was well known and his de facto partisanship was obvious. The *Christian Century* welcomed Kennedy's inauguration day "as marking the end of Protestantism as a national religion and its advent as the distinctive faith of a creative minority,"[41] but evangelical vices were having none of that compromise.

Moreover, evangelicals had no intention of immersing themselves, through a grand series of mergers, into some megachurch led by the despised liberals. The culture of their own neighborhoods demanded vigorous defense, they believed, rather than the critical reassessments generated by sympathetic appreciation of other cultures. The evangelicals came to support Israel on grounds highly problematic even for ecumenical allies of Israel: the gathering of Jews in Israel was said to be a step toward the "second coming of Christ." The ostensibly biblical basis (Deuteronomy 30:1–5 promised the Jews a homeland before the appearance of the Messiah) for this closer alliance with American Zionists was thoroughly Christian-centered and bore no meaningful relationship to the ecumenical welcoming of secular as well as religious Jews as full partners in American life.[42]

All these signs of provinciality seemed to mark evangelicals as destined for oblivion.

Hence, the mainline cadres entered the battles of the sixties with imperfect intelligence. They failed to measure the strength of the forces carrying Graham from triumph to triumph. The ecumenical leaders also greatly underestimated the appeals of secular ideas and communities. Ecumenical Protestantism, flanked by a formidable opponent within the community of faith and hemorrhaging troops who deserted the ranks to vanish in the secular ether, lost its prominent place in the United States, perhaps forever.

6

The 1960s and the Decline
of the Mainline

We have lost the South for a generation.

—LYNDON JOHNSON, 1964

ECUMENICAL PROTESTANTISM began the 1960s with an
unprecedented spasm of collective self-interrogation, often
touching on self-flagellation. While evangelical leaders were
encouraging their tribe to increase pride in their own tightly
knit communities and to double down on their ostensibly clear
and stable faith, their mainline counterparts were giving hell to
ecumenical churchgoers for being slow to modernize. In one
scorching critique after another, ecumenical intellectuals accused privileged white Christians of avoiding the social and
political implications of the gospel and of being prisoners to
ideas long since discredited by modern learning. A new cohort
of ecumenical polemicists had been deeply affected by the missionary witness to the world's diversity and its inequalities. This
cohort sided with anticolonial movements in the Global South,
embraced Jews as full partners in creating a more just America,

and expressed strong support for the church-centered African American struggle against white supremacy. These ecumenical intellectuals opened to full bore the engines of the campaign for a more cosmopolitan Protestantism.

In *My People Is the Enemy: An Autobiographical Polemic* (1964), an Episcopal layman who spent seven years living amid poverty in Harlem while serving as a lawyer to indigent Black people excoriated his fellow white Christians for failing to confront racial and economic inequality. "The churches of white society in America have largely forfeited any claim to leadership" in tackling these evils, William Stringfellow complained, while offering page after page of earnest instruction on how a truly Christian approach, as he understood it, would engage a color-defined population still not incorporated as fully American. In *The Suburban Captivity of the Churches* (1961), Gibson Winter of the University of Chicago Divinity School challenged Christians to go beyond their sheltered lives and address the panorama of injustice that surrounded them.[1] Economic justice, downplayed during the 1950s, returned with a vengeance in the new round of manifestos. Adamantly universalist, these writings addressed the injustices suffered by particular groups within a presumably single moral, religious, and national community.

Although the missionary project had already been substantially reformed, this group of writers complained that the colonialist-imperialist past remained a serious impediment to missionary success even as a service enterprise. In *The Unpopular Missionary* (1964), Ralph E. Dodge, a senior Methodist missionary to Angola and Rhodesia, warned that if the American churches did not turn more control and resources over to the Indigenous churches, missions were doomed to go the way of colonial governments: out for good, and for the same reasons.

The basic problem was that the missionary project was still hesitant to accept Indigenous peoples on their own terms as *"human beings"* and as "full brothers in Jesus Christ"—not as copies of Christians in Memphis and Minneapolis. The church, he wrote, "must reject categorically all attitudes and practices of racial superiority."[2] James A. Scherer, a Lutheran missionary to China, sounded the same notes of anger and warning in *Missionary, Go Home! A Reappraisal of the Christian World Mission* (1964).[3] Wilfred Cantwell Smith, a former missionary to India, warned Christians that they had yet to sufficiently renounce their inherited notions of spiritual and racial superiority; they must recognize that they were just one group among many. Human life henceforth was to be "cast in a multicultural context," he insisted, employing the term *multicultural* three decades before it became popular.[4]

The most widely discussed books in this polemical package were more ambitiously theological and yet more radical. Gabriel Vahanian's *The Death of God: The Culture of Our Post-Christian Era* (1961) and Paul M. Van Buren's *The Secular Meaning of the Gospel* (1963) established the vogue of the "death of God theologians."[5] But these departures from the traditional supernaturalism of the average churchgoer were tame compared with *Honest to God* (1963), by Anglican bishop John A. T. Robinson. Although written in England by a clergyman best known at the time for his court testimony against the censorship of D. H. Lawrence's *Lady Chatterley's Lover*, this colloquially phrased manifesto gained instant notoriety in the United States, well beyond the seminaries. Robinson attacked as hopelessly anachronistic the ideas about God and Jesus that were common among Christians, mocking the mystifications that suggest "that Jesus was really God almighty walking about on earth, dressed up as a man . . . taking part in a charade."[6] Much of Robinson's message was already incorporated into the discourse of liberal seminaries as a result of the calls for "demythologized" and "religionless" Christianity made somewhat cryptically by theologians Rudolf Bultmann, Dietrich Bonhoeffer, and Paul Tillich. But Robinson's breakaway best seller popularized as never before the strivings of a theological elite to update Christian teachings in relation to contemporary culture and modern, scientific standards of truth. For a prominent cleric to characterize as downright dishonest the sincere God talk of the average churchgoer exposed as never before the gap between the people in the pew and the increasingly cosmopolitan church leaders.

Robinson and his champions were quick to insist that the Christian faith was just as true as ever, once properly understood. Among the ecumenical leaders who hailed the book was John C. Bennett, who called its publication "A Most Welcome Event."[7] Still, many of Robinson's colleagues condemned the book as dangerously misleading because of its sensational vocabulary. This debate was ostensibly intramural for believers, but it undoubtedly diminished the credibility of the specific beliefs that Robinson attacked (for example, the notion of a God "out there") more than it enhanced the credibility of the beliefs he defended (for example, God is our "ground of being"). Taking to a new extreme a classic impulse in ecumenical Protestantism to engage the world rather than to withdraw from it, Robinson dramatically legitimized the diverse world of contemporary culture as an arena for sympathetic engagement, not to be held at a biblically warranted distance. Robinson made the generic ideal of honesty, rather than any specifically Christian doctrine, the touchstone for his testimony, and he blurred the line between what most people took Christianity to be, and the enlightened, humane dispositions of the left-liberal intelligentsia.

Two years later, a young American Baptist minister pressed the same line of thought in a more carefully argued book. Harvey Cox's manifesto, *The Secular City* (1965), made the case for a politically engaged religion organized around human responsibility for the destiny of a world that many Christians wrongly assumed to be in God's hands. The book soon sold more than one million copies. Cox celebrated "secularization" as a liberation from "all supernatural myths and sacred symbols." While insisting that God was no less present throughout secular domains than within what traditionalists called "religion," Cox concluded with the extraordinary suggestion that the very name of God was so misleading that it might make sense to stop mentioning God altogether until our worldly experience gives us a new vocabulary. "Like Moses," he wrote in the book's concluding sentence, let us be "confident that we will be granted a new name by events of the future." But for now, he concluded, "we must simply take up the work of liberating the captives."[8]

Cox doubted that the average provincial Christian was equipped to deal with the wider world that the theologians had come to master, and which they had an obligation to explain to the faithful. "Secularization" took place "only when the cosmopolitan confrontations of city living exposed the relativity of the myths and traditions" once thought to be "unquestionable." Convinced of the virtues of "heterogeneity" and "the color and character lent by diversity," Cox pressed the case for "pluralism and tolerance" throughout the world, but especially in the United States, where the recent "emancipation of Catholics, Jews, and others" from "an enforced Protestant cultural religion" boded well for further diversification. "It would be too bad," Cox reflected, "if Catholics and Jews, having rightly pushed for the de-Protestantizing of American society and having in effect won, should now join Protestants in reconstituting a kind of tripartite American religion. . . . At this point, Christians should support the secularization of American society, recognizing that secularists, atheists, and agnostics do not have to be second-class citizens."[9]

Cox and the other writers of this early 1960s ecumenical effusion condemned the failings of their own churches without apparent fear. Their radicalism could also be construed as an attack on the ideas and practices of evangelicals, even guiltier, it would seem, than the ecumenical rank and file of the errors these polemicists exposed. But these polemics were not aimed at the evangelical party; rather, they were directed against the liberalizers for not liberalizing enough, for failing to press yet harder the campaign to achieve a more cosmopolitan Protestantism. While Billy Graham was making Christianity simpler and more accessible, the ecumenical intelligentsia was making it more demanding.

The self-assured, if not complacent ecumenical leadership took increasingly forthright and controversial stands on issues of the day.[10] Mainliners were among the earliest and most vociferous opponents of the American military action in Vietnam. This was a particularly sharp point of tension with evangelicals, the overwhelming majority of whom wanted nothing to do with the antiwar activities of the liberals. The NCC supported Palestinian independence from Israel, endorsed the resumption of normal relations with Cuba, put money and legal resources behind the United Farm Workers of America, rallied to support the American Indian Movement during the siege at Wounded Knee, and took sides with Soviet-backed African insurgents against Portuguese colonial regimes. Impatient with the parochialism of denominational cultures, top church officials, including Presbyterian Eugene Carson Blake and Episcopalian James Pike, called for massive mergers eventuating, perhaps, in a single, unified Protestant church for the United States and even for the world. Blake was way out front on the matter of Jim Crow and was arrested at a civil rights demonstration in Maryland in 1963, the same year the *Christian Century* published Martin Luther King Jr.'s "Letter from Birmingham Jail."

The ecumenical-evangelical divide as it existed in 1963 was on full display that August when Billy Graham, asked to comment on the "I Have a Dream" speech King delivered at the March on Washington, was candid about evangelical priorities. "Little white children of Alabama will walk hand in hand with little Black children," Graham explained in crisp and clear language, "only when Christ comes again."[11] No one etched more vividly the political coordinates of the ecumenical-evangelical divide at that historical moment.[12]

Ecumenical support for the Civil Rights Movement of the 1960s was a pivotal event in the campaign for a more cosmopolitan Protestantism. King's national stature was greater than anything achieved by previous Black leaders supported by the FCC and the NCC. Benjamin Mays, Channing Tobias, and Howard Thurman were not household names for the white public, and the initiatives they led, however courageous and heroic, were not at the center of American politics. King's actions, however, were so much at the center that it became common for historians to refer to his time as "the King Years."[13]

With the coming of King, African American churches became a more important, integral part of ecumenical Protestantism. When the ecumenical leadership created the Consultation on Church Union, the structure within which denominational representatives were to meet to talk over the possibilities of actually creating a single, national Protestant church, three of the nine most involved denominations were African American. Although the representatives of the Black denominations reminded the white delegates of the economic inequality among the various churches and asked that resources be redistributed, the very fact of their involvement marked the desire of the white officials to find a way to integrate the churches ethnoracially as well as doctrinally and signaled how distant the ecumenical leaders were from their evangelical counterparts.

The Consultation on Church Union eventually failed for many reasons, especially the refusal of churchgoers and their pastors to give up their long-standing identities and structures of authority. The venture foundered also because the conferees could not agree about what amounted to reparations for the Black churches. Evangelical periodicals attacked the liberalizers for substituting politics for religion. FBI director J. Edgar Hoover, a key ally of white evangelicals in the struggle to maintain a broadly Christian-infused regime of white supremacy, published a series of articles in *Christianity Today* charging that the liberal church preachers and officials were serving the interests of the Soviet Union.[14]

Rank-and-file white churchgoers in ecumenical churches were aware of these critiques and sometimes worried about them. Had their own Methodist and Presbyterian and Episcopalian leaders become too radical, not only on race, but on Vietnam and a host of other issues? The gap between the cosmopolitan leadership and the provincial laity (and many small-town and rural pastors) within ecumenical churches widened.[15] Church officials found themselves increasingly on the defensive in national and regional governance bodies. The people in the pews and many of their pastors refused to approve funding for projects they did not like. The budget of the NCC nosedived in the 1970s. Employees had to be laid off.

And just then, at exactly this late 1960s, early 1970s moment, the ecumenical denominations began their much-discussed

decline in membership. The experience was all the more striking since it got going just after church membership had reached
all-time highs and was expected to grow further as more and
more upwardly mobile evangelicals would join the mainline
denominations. But instead the Northern Presbyterians (northern and southern Presbyterian denominations did not become
United Presbyterians until 1983) lost nearly 20 percent of their
members between 1965 and 1975. Episcopalians reached their
highest numbers in 1967, but by 1975 had lost about 9 percent.
The Methodists' zenith was 1964, but they then lost 11 percent
of their membership in the next decade and by the end of the
century were down 28 percent.[16] The United Church of Christ
had more than two million members in 1957, when it was
formed through a merger of the Congregationalists and the
German Reformed, but sixty years later it had 850,000, a decline
of 63 percent. As late as 1976 the seven denominations known
as the core of the mainline still could count 31 percent of the
nation's population as members, but only a dozen years later
they could claim only 19 percent. By 2018, membership in the
same denominations had dropped to about 12 percent of the
national population.[17]

What happened?

Did people move from ecumenical to evangelical churches?
Yes, some did. About 10 percent of self-identified evangelicals
in the 1970s had once been members of mainline denominations.[18] But this migration was not nearly enough to explain the
magnitude of the ecumenical decline. Several other factors were
more decisive.

Increasing numbers of children reared in ecumenical congregations decided during their teens or twenties not to affiliate with the churches of their parents. Liberalizing church
leaders were pushing their campaign too far and too fast for

some of their older members, but not far and fast enough for many young people who were attentive to the cultural and political movements around them. Ecumenical parents were likely to encourage their children to explore the world and make their own decisions about it. They did just that, and they took advantage of the expanding opportunities to form communities beyond the churches. Young people departed their natal churches in droves. Evangelical parents, by contrast, encouraged their children to be leery of the world beyond their own communities and eventually became heavily committed to homeschooling.

The migration of young people out of ecumenical churches followed in part from the unprecedented growth and prestige of higher education. Never before had so many young people gone to college, and never before had campuses presented such a dynamic, multifaceted, and attractive setting for youthful experimentation. Sociologists and journalists reported that academia was where the action was, politically, intellectually, and spiritually. "There has fallen to the universities a unique, indispensable, and capital function in the intellectual and spiritual life of modern society," the famous writer and political commentator Walter Lippmann wrote in the *New Republic* in 1966. Cultural leadership belongs to the academy "rather than, let us say, to the churches or the government," Lippmann explained, because our scientists and scholars have proven to be our most reliable authorities for understanding "the nature of good and evil" and for showing us how "to ascertain and to recognize the truth and to distinguish it from error."[19]

The domain of higher education, unsurprisingly, was more directly influenced by both Jewish and missionary cosmopolitanism than any other institutional segment of American life. In teaching and in research, professors extensively engaged the world beyond the North Atlantic West. Undergraduate curricula, doctoral programs, and disciplinary professional associations all made Asian societies, especially, more familiar to those in the orbit of higher education. Jewish Americans were well represented in the classrooms and in university governance. Higher education was the single most culturally strategic space for these two demographic transformations of American society to register. On campuses, missionary cosmopolitanism and Jewish cosmopolitanism converged as nowhere else.

Sociologist Robert Wuthnow's classic account of the impact of education on the ecumenical-evangelical divide rings true after more than three decades: "It was the better educated, both among laity and clergy, who pushed religious organizations in a more socially activist direction, first in the civil rights movement and then in the protest movement against the Vietnam War. These were the persons who came to favor greater cooperation between the different faiths and denominations, who registered lower levels of prejudice and misgiving toward members of other faiths, and who themselves were more likely to switch denominations, to visit other denominations, and to marry outside of their own faith tradition."[20]

Evangelicals were correct to identify universities as threats to interests they held dear. Christianity, so long protected from rigorous scrutiny in American classrooms, was losing its authority. Summarizing a three-year workshop on religion and higher education sponsored by the Lilly Foundation in the late 1990s, philosopher Nicholas Wolterstorff noted with some disbelief that so many of his colleagues, heirs to the most hegemonic cultural project in the entire history of the North Atlantic West, had become convinced that "Christians, both faculty and students, are being victimized *on account of* their Christianity."[21]

Registering the increased cultural importance of college campuses, ecumenical churches increased the financing that enabled denominationally sponsored campus ministries to expand their services. Yet, as Dorothy Bass shows, these campus ministries were caught between the priorities of their denominational sponsors and the tendency of their student constituencies to embrace radical ideas that were hard to reconcile with an attachment to organized Christianity. William Stringfellow, Harvey Cox, and their kind encouraged young Protestants to think beyond the church, practice their faith in the world, and even allow the church to disappear as the inherited faith flourished in full commerce with the world. "Only when we in the church are willing to lose our institutional life in love for and service to the world," one Bonhoeffer-inspired ecumenical youth proclaimed, "will we deliver the nature of our true life, our mission, and our Lord."[22]

While many young people were leaving the ecumenical churches, those who remained were having fewer babies. During the baby boom that affected most of American society, Northern Presbyterian women gave birth to only an average of 1.6 children, while the overwhelmingly stay-at-home evangelical women gave birth to an average of 2.4 children—more babies than even Catholic women delivered during the same years. Ecumenical families that favored family planning soon had fewer children, and as those children grew up, quite a few departed. Those who remained had fewer children than their parents. As a consequence, the proportion of church members over the age of fifty grew rapidly. The graying of ecumenical churches is easily measured. In 1957, only 36 percent of Lutherans were over fifty, yet by 1983, 45 percent were. During that same quarter century, the percentage of Methodists over fifty increased from 40 to 49 percent, and the percentage of Episcopalians over fifty increased from 36 to 46 percent.[23] The churches contained fewer and fewer women of child-bearing age.[24]

Birth rates do not exist in cultural vacuums. Ecumenicals encouraged contraception and were more comfortable with women joining the workforce than were evangelicals. Even before World War II ecumenical churches not only supported sex education in the public schools but were largely responsible for developing it as part of standard curricula. Evangelicals generally disapproved. According to sex education's leading historian, the topic was essentially a subset of "the story of liberal Protestants in the United States."[25] In the 1940s, Alfred Kinsey found theologically liberal clergy to be among the most committed defenders of his research on sexual behavior. Support for the legalization of abortion was widespread among ecumenical leaders well before the *Roe v. Wade* decision of 1973. Liberal ideas about sex were central to the ecumenical-evangelical divide as it deepened in the late 1940s and 1950s.[26] Evangelical families not only managed to keep more of their children close to home than did ecumenical parents; they had more children to begin with.

No less important as a cause of the decline in ecumenical church membership was the growing reluctance of upwardly mobile evangelicals to join. The postwar increase in ecumenical churchgoers in the suburbs had been based largely on upward class mobility: Nazarenes, Adventists, and members of other evangelical confessions "moved up" to the Presbyterians and Methodists as they prospered and gained more education. But by the end of the 1960s, oil money, media expansion, and enterprise had made evangelical Protestantism sufficiently respectable that one did not have to leave it in order to be recognized as an established part of American society. No longer did one have to be mainline to be mainstream. Joining the ecumenical churches, moreover, obliged one to face intensifying pressure to take a stand against white supremacy and to abandon the notion of a "Christian America," and to put aside inherited ideas about the Bible.

Evangelical churches made it easy to resist such pressures. An evangelical could be counted as fully Christian without taking on potentially unwelcome social obligations. What did Billy Graham mean by "accepting Christ"? It could mean remaining within the confines of the inherited culture depicted in Norman Rockwell's *Saturday Evening Post* covers while simply promising to be better at it. To be better, that is, at living up to that culture's self-image. Practicing the Golden Rule, being faithful to one's spouse, eschewing pornography and same-sex intimacy, avoiding the abuse of alcohol and drugs, extending a helping hand to less well-off neighbors, praying on a daily basis, and supporting the essentials of the American economic and political order until its injustices were corrected by changes in the human heart were not necessarily signs of God's grace. But these behaviors were expected of those who came to Graham's altar. That was enough.

It was far from enough for the ecumenical leaders, especially in the wake of the withering self-scrutiny the polemicists of the early 1960s had forced upon them. Ecumenical officialdom demanded more from the faithful. This demand rendered the historical situation of ecumenical Protestantism comparable to that of the Democratic Party when it endorsed the cause of civil rights for African Americans in 1964. "We have lost the South for a generation," President Lyndon Johnson was quoted as remarking at that pivotal moment. At stake was not only the standing of African Americans—the crucial issue for the Democrats—but also the entire campaign for a more cosmopolitan Protestantism, including perspectives on empire, sex, gender, and the critical approach to scripture and the supernatural popularized by writers like Cox and Robinson.

Ecumenical leaders were less attuned than Johnson to the risks they were taking, but they, too, believed that the time had come to redirect the institutions and constituencies they led. Hence they abandoned to opportunistic evangelicals the classic missionary goal of conversion, the powerful claim of a proprietary relationship to the American nation, and a host of other aspirations to which many white Americans remained attached. In pursuit of causes they believed were inspired by God, ecumenical leaders encouraged secular alliances that blurred the boundaries of their faith community and risked the gradual loss of their children to secular communities. They accommodated perspectives on women and the family that reduced their capacity to reproduce themselves exactly at the same critical moment in history that they espoused positions on race, empire, and divinity that diminished their ability to recruit new members from the ranks of evangelicals. Just as the Democrats lost most of the South to the Republicans—and for a much longer time than Johnson himself expected—the ecumenicals lost to evangelicals more and more of the authority to speak for Protestantism.

The campaign for a more cosmopolitan Protestantism lacked a single, dramatic moment like the one Johnson memorialized in his famous remark about the South. But the dynamic was the same. The people in charge of an enterprise decided it was time to do things very differently and risked losing a major segment of the enterprise's traditional constituency. The similarity between the two cases is visible even in the third decade of the twenty-first century, when Democrats still struggle to win the

support of white voters, especially in the South, and ecumenical Protestants still struggle to retain a substantial amount of the symbolic capital of Christianity.

The Republican Party's subsequent embrace of the "Southern Strategy" makes the analogy of ecumenical Protestantism to the Democratic Party all the more instructive. Historians do not agree on just how central this strategy was in the thinking of President Richard Nixon and his advisors in the early 1970s, but there is no doubt that it was part of the mix.[27] By mobilizing the voters least comfortable with the ending of the old racial order, Republicans understood the potential consequences for the Electoral College: if they could lock in the South and tighten their control of the rural midwestern and Mountain states, where they already had a strong hand, little else was needed to win the presidency. One or two of the more urban midwestern states—perhaps Ohio—would clinch it. The same idea applied to the US Senate. The Republicans did continue through the end of the twentieth century to appeal to suburban whites in the urban Northeast and in California, but the gravitational pull of the reliable white voters of the South gradually defined the Republican Party and made the Southern Strategy a central feature of American politics.

What made the Southern Strategy possible is what we continue to call "race" (the visible marks of physical descent, popularly understood), not religion. But that strategy was an event in American religious as well as racial history. Evangelicals dominated the church-intensive states of the old Confederacy, where ecumenicals were the weakest. This had been true for generations and was resoundingly confirmed in 2014 when the Public Religion Research Institute found that white evangelicals composed more than a quarter of the population in fifteen

states, eight of which had belonged to the Confederacy (Alabama, Arkansas, Georgia, Mississippi, North Carolina, South
Carolina, Tennessee, and Texas). The most extreme case was
Tennessee, where 43 percent of residents were white evangelicals. Two of the other fifteen had been slave states without joining the Confederacy (Kentucky and Missouri), and two others
(Oklahoma and West Virginia) were adjacent to Confederate
states. The other five were scattered in the prairies and the
mountains (Indiana, Kansas, Montana, South Dakota, and
Wyoming).[28]

An additional fact contributed to the religious character of
the Southern Strategy. The ecumenical churches that did exist
in the South were decidedly more conservative than those in
the North, the Midwest, and the West. Denominational officers
and leaders of transdenominational organizations were con-
tinually frustrated by the reluctance of their southern affiliates
to accept policies and programs that the national bodies had
agreed upon. The white Methodists, Presbyterians, and Disciples of Christ in the southern states were closer to their evangelical neighbors than their counterparts in other sections of
the country were to theirs. The southern ecumenicals voted
more like the evangelicals than not. For example, the southern
Presbyterians, although affiliated with the National Council of
Churches, rejected pressures to merge their own pre–Civil War
denomination until 1983, when the United Presbyterian
Church, at the urging of former missionaries, brought into one
organization the sectional bodies created in 1861.

The Republican Party's pursuit of the Southern Strategy
resulted in the gradual but ever tightening connection between Republicans and white evangelicals. The two-party
system of the Protestants became more entwined than ever
before with the two-party system of American politics. As

white evangelicals became more Republican, African American Protestants and white ecumenicals became more identified with the Democratic Party. So, too, did the rapidly increasing numbers of religiously unaffiliated Americans. This sharpened ethnoreligious polarization became an enduring feature of American public life.

7

Ecumenical Democrats, Evangelical Republicans, and Post-Protestants

Now, it is a disgraceful and dangerous thing for an infidel to hear a Christian, presumably giving the meaning of Holy Scripture, talking nonsense. . . . Reckless and incompetent expounders of Holy Scripture bring untold trouble and sorrow on their wiser brethren when they are caught in one of their mischievous false opinions and are taken to task by those who are not bound by the authority of our sacred books. For then, to defend their utterly foolish and obviously untrue statements, they will try to call upon Holy Scripture for proof and even recite from memory many passages which they think support their position, although they understand neither what they say nor the things about which they make assertion.

—AUGUSTINE OF HIPPO, 410

SENATOR JOSH HAWLEY gained attention for his fist-raised support of the pro-Trump mob's attack the Capitol on January 6, 2021. The Missouri Republican left no doubt about the character of his religious faith and its relation to American politics. He insisted in a speech of 2017 that Christians must take the authority of Christ "into the public realm," "to seek the obedience" of all the nations, including "our nation." He continued, "There is not one square inch of all creation of which Jesus Christ is not Lord." The destiny of the American nation, Hawley explained, was Christian, or must be made so: the "ultimate authority" of Jesus Christ must be taken "into every sphere of life."[1] How different from the ecumenical theorist Wilfred Cantwell Smith's insistence in 1960 that Christians were just one group among many and that they must accept their diminished role in a multicultural future.[2]

The Republican Party, in Hawley's construction, is an instrument to advance the dominion of Christianity, not a partner of the country's other major party in the practice of democracy. Religious authority "takes captive" the political.[3]

The support for Trump by white evangelicals like Hawley is the culmination of decades of Republican Party cultivation of this particular ethnoreligious group. Well before January 6, 2021, the Republican Party had written off the sections of the country with the highest education levels and the greatest demographic diversity and had come to rest its fortunes on white voters who were slower to welcome nonwhites into equal citizenship. These targeted voters were also more religious and less educated. Josh Hawley went to Stanford and Yale, but most of the evangelicals who agreed with Hawley did not have the educational advantages he had.

The Democratic Party, in the meantime, became more than ever a home for voters of a very different kind. African Americans, especially, were overwhelmingly Democrats. The Democrats could count on highly educated Americans of all ethnicities. People without any religious affiliation were also much more

often Democrats than not. Not all Democrats fit these catego-
ries, just as not all Republicans were white evangelicals. But
these were the most reliable constituencies of each political
party, and each was reminded regularly by the press of their
own identities and of the expected political coordinates.

Race was at the center of this dialectical polarization. Since
the 1960s, the Southern Strategy of the Republican Party has
played successfully to the sentiments of white voters who were
uncomfortable with the Civil Rights Movement and with its
ecumenical supporters.

Ronald Reagan resoundingly vindicated the Southern Strategy and its heavily evangelical foundation. He opened his suc-
cessful 1980 presidential campaign by defending "states' rights"
in Neshoba County, Mississippi, standing virtually on the
graves of James Chaney, Andrew Goodman, and Michael
Schwerner, the three voting rights organizers murdered by the
Ku Klux Klan in 1964. Reagan then won thunderous applause
a few weeks later at a convention of fifteen thousand evangelicals when he declared, "I know you can't endorse me, but I
endorse you." As president, Reagan did not always throw his
weight behind specific evangelical policy proposals. But he
presented himself as their champion and was largely accepted
as such. His mantra that "government is the problem" reso-
nated with white southerners who were prepared to set aside
their antipathy to federal power—inherited from the defense
of slavery and of Jim Crow—only when it was clear, as it had
been during the New Deal, that Black people would be largely
excluded from the federally funded economic and social ben-
efits at issue.

Ironically, the former California governor's victory was
achieved at the expense of an actual white southerner who was,
theologically, a bona fide, born-again evangelical: Jimmy

Carter. During Carter's presidency the federal government had begun to challenge the tax-exempt status of the racially segregated private schools that proliferated in southern states in the wake of the Supreme Court's rulings in *Brown v. Board of Education I and II* (1954, 1955) that deemed racial segregation of public schools to be unconstitutional and ordered such segregation ended "with all deliberate speed." What kind of southerner was the peanut-farming Sunday school teacher from Georgia? Less trustworthy, it turned out, than the slick Hollywood actor. Defenders of the schools in question argued that the enforcement of antidiscrimination laws was actually an attack on the constitutional right to free exercise of religion.

It was a great opportunity, as historian Randall Balmer summarizes, "to shift the terms of the debate from a defense of racial discrimination in evangelical institutions to a supposed defense of religious liberty, all the while conveniently ignoring the fact that tax exemption is a form of public subsidy." Suddenly, evangelicalism, "arguably the most influential social and religious movement in American history, adopted the posture of a persecuted minority" under assault from a "secular majority."[4]

Although the free exercise claim did not succeed with specific regard to racial segregation, it gained more traction in subsequent decades when evangelical institutions and businesses joined Catholic and other religiously affiliated hospitals to seek exemptions from the requirement that they provide full reproductive health care and serve gays and lesbians.

Casting about for other issues with which to attract white evangelicals, especially in states where the defense of racial segregation was not a priority, Republican politicians settled on abortion. Until the 1970s abortion had been largely a Catholic issue, and even five years after *Roe v. Wade* (1973), "pro-life" advocacy remained tepid. A majority of Protestants, ecumenical and evangelical, generally accepted *Roe* while supporting some restrictions on access to abortion for adolescents. Yet as Paul Weyrich and other Reagan advisors sensed, the issue had potential appeal to evangelicals who were protective of traditional gender roles. They mobilized luminaries Francis Schaeffer and Phyllis Schlafly (who was Catholic, but proved to be an effective ally) to promote antiabortion efforts.

The initiative worked, despite its dubious scriptural warrant. The Hebrew Bible includes dozens of explicit rules for personal conduct, none of which address abortion. The Reagan campaign did not see fit to call into political service any of the other items in this formidable inventory of Old Testament rules. The New Testament is entirely silent on abortion.[5] Yet a religious community committed to literal readings of the Bible, once it became persuaded that traditional family roles and hierarchies were threatened by the legalization of abortion, was suddenly comfortable with bold, new extrapolations from scripture. It was routinely claimed, for example, that a fetus's status as a human being was established by Luke 1:15: "He will be filled with the Holy Spirit, even from his mother's womb." Another popular "proof text" was Jeremiah 1:5: "Before I formed you in the womb I knew you, before you were born I set you apart; I appointed you as a prophet to the nations."

Republican politicians took advantage of this novel opportunity and became "pro-life." Reagan himself had supported women's reproductive rights in California but joined other Republicans with no previous record of opposition to abortion in changing sides. Southern Baptist leaders who had never before identified abortion as an issue now pivoted against it. Hence the antiabortion movement, as Reva Siegel, Linda Greenhouse, and others have documented, appeared late in the day.[6] The evangelical-centered opposition to abortion by the Republican

Party was not focused on the South, but the preponderance there of evangelicals made antiabortion a structural supplement to the Southern Strategy, rendering that strategy more religious in character than it otherwise would have been.

When Republican presidential candidates risked losing white evangelical voters, they took decisive, public steps to neutralize the threat. In 1988, George H. W. Bush faced a primary challenge from the evangelical preacher Pat Robertson. The Bush campaign's notorious "Willie Horton" ad, accusing Democrat Michael Dukakis of being "soft on crime," was designed to appeal to evangelical voters in southern states. It was an unabashedly "race-baiting TV production," notes historian Anthea Butler, featuring "a prisoner who had raped a white Maryland woman and bound and stabbed her boyfriend while on furlough during Dukakis's term as governor of Massachusetts."[7] It greatly strengthened Bush's candidacy. A dozen years later, when George W. Bush faced probable defeat in another Republican primary by John McCain, the younger Bush made a highly publicized visit to fundamentalist Bob Jones University and promoted the rumor that McCain had fathered an illegitimate Black daughter.

When McCain himself wanted to shore up evangelical support in his 2008 campaign against Democrat Barack Obama, he chose the extreme evangelical Sarah Palin as his running mate. Palin caused McCain some trouble with nonevangelical voters, but she cemented McCain's evangelical support. McCain's choice of Palin also advanced the Republican Party's increasing dependence on the kind of voter who could appreciate a genuine premillennial dispensationalist. Palin was the most theologically radical individual ever to run for president or vice president on a major party's ticket.

Thus evangelical support for Republicans was far from new in the era of Donald Trump. Nearly the same percentage of evangelicals that voted for Trump had voted for McCain in 2008 and for Mitt Romney in 2012. But some things were different. In 2016 and 2020 evangelicals embraced a man whose personal character was obviously at variance with evangelical teachings. This was not something Romney, McCain, or George W. Bush demanded of evangelicals. Novel, too, was the extent of Trump's disdain for highly educated voters on the two coasts. In neither of his presidential campaigns did Trump make a serious effort to win votes in the entire Eastern Corridor, from Maine to Virginia, with the exception of Pennsylvania. He also ignored the Pacific Coast states of California, Oregon, and Washington. Already by 2016, to be sure, the pre-Trump Republican Party's gradual abandonment of those fifteen coastal states was so far advanced that Susan Collins of Maine and Patrick Toomey of Pennsylvania were the only Republicans among the thirty senators representing those fifteen states.

Some evangelical intellectuals insisted that Trump's clerical apologists are not true evangelicals at all. "It should be easy to see that is a mistake," declared George M. Marsden in 2019, "to generalize about evangelicals on the basis of the behavior of white American Trump voters."[8] Evangelicalism is best seen, argued David W. Bebbington, as a coherent system of four interlocking doctrinal commitments: "Biblicism" (reliance on the Bible itself), "conversionism" (the need to covert others to the faith), "crucicentrism" (a focus on the "atonement," the idea that Christ's death on the cross atoned for the sins of humankind), and "activism" (the idea that action in the world must reflect the gospel).

This "quadrilateral," as Bebbington and his scholarly allies call this set of beliefs, has some value for understanding the doctrinal history of at least part of evangelicalism across the centuries. But this sense of "true" evangelicalism elides the entire history of fundamentalist and evangelical connections with business-friendly individualism. Missing, too, from the quadrilateral is the vibrant tradition of premillennial dispensationalism, according to which evangelicals were encouraged to accept wildly implausible ideas, making QAnon's theories seem less strange than they otherwise would be.[9] And even when we take seriously these "four tenets of evangelical orthodoxy," observes historian Amanda Porterfield, "they operate together as a defense against skeptical inquiry" and thus fit in perfectly with the Republican Party of Donald Trump.[10]

Kristin Kobes Du Mez shows how little the quadrilateral did to protect American democracy from Trump and just how far that quadrilateral has been from the minds of most evangelical churchgoers. Those minds have been filled, instead, with a deeply anti-intellectual, Manichean, and persistently misogynist "evangelical culture of consumption." Setting aside theological complexities, this culture embraces, as Du Mez puts it, "militant masculinity, an ideology that enshrines patriarchal authority and condones the callous display of power, at home and abroad. By the time Trump arrived proclaiming himself their savior, conservative white evangelicals had already traded a faith that privileges humility and elevates 'the least of these' for one that derides gentleness as the provinces of wusses. . . . In reality, evangelicals did not cast their vote despite their beliefs, but because of them."[11]

Hence, while it is a mistake to assume that evangelical culture itself lacks any resources for honest engagement with the truth about American politics, it is a yet more egregious error to downplay the strain of tribal authoritarianism in evangelical culture, and it is an equally egregious error to ignore how much that strain owes to ideas about epistemic authority preached decade after decade by evangelical preachers and writers.

In 2010, two leading social scientists concluded on the basis of extensive research that about three-quarters of the Americans whom scholars count as the most religious "reject evolution altogether, and believe instead that God created human beings fewer than ten thousand years ago."[12] There is no mystery about where the faithful got these ideas, and no uncertainty as to what groups of clergy were in a position to disabuse churchgoers of their illusions. If "distrust of scientists has become part of cultural identity, of what it means to be white and evangelical in America," as the *New York Times* commented in 2021, this outcome owes much to purveyors of "the Christian worldview," a phase uncommon among ecumenical Protestants but ubiquitous among evangelicals.[13]

Evangelical intellectuals developed the concept of "the Christian worldview," historian Molly Worthen explains, as "a powerful rhetorical strategy" that "curtails debate, justifies hardline politics, and discourages sympathetic voters from entertaining moderation or compromise."[14] Evangelicals committed to the notion of an "inerrant" Bible struggled with uncertainties about just what inerrant biblical authority could mean. Disagreement within orthodoxy was a problem for a tradition of biblical hermeneutics according to which achieving an accurate understanding of the Word was simply, as Marsden explains, a matter of "taking the hard facts of Scripture, carefully arranging and classifying them, and thus discovering the clear patterns which Scripture revealed."[15] Countless preachers assured the faithful that the Bible "means what it says and says what it means." It was dangerous to identify ambiguities and to confront the fact that the earliest known texts that make up New Testament are thousands of manuscripts, with multiple differences between them. The Bible contains, after all, more than thirty thousand verses composed by a great many authors over the course of many centuries. Only an extravagantly mystical conception of the Bible can endow it with a clear and unchanging message.

The "Christian worldview" was a way to circumvent this epistemic morass and to avoid sectarian conflicts within the community of faith. The concept was amorphous enough to resist detailed critical interrogation, yet could be invoked with sufficient conviction to keep evangelicals on the same page and to serve them in disputes with nonevangelicals. All secular knowledge lacked genuine authority; rather, each claim had to be assessed within "Christian" or "biblical" presuppositions. The concept of the "Christian worldview" denied authority to any truth claim that had not been assessed in an ostensibly Christian perspective. The Manichean tendencies of the Fundamentalist movement were thus perpetuated and renewed. You were in the know, or you were not. Worthen locates the development of the "Christian worldview" in the context of evangelicalism's long established "pattern of hostility and ambivalence toward the standards of tolerance, logic, and evidence by which most secular thinkers in the West have agreed to abide." Universities were a special challenge, but for evangelicals "academic freedom as understood in the modern secular university," Worthen adds, "was not freedom at all, but slavery to human pride that would lead young Christians from the narrow path."[16]

No wonder millions of evangelicals were an easy mark for Donald Trump, willing to believe his Twitter stream of falsehoods. Political scientists found that at the time of the 2020 election, "white evangelicals" believed "more often than not" that "the Democrats are part of a vast criminal conspiracy not just working against Trump but against the interest and rights of Christians," that Trump "has been anointed by God to serve them," and that "the United States is a Christian nation whose success is part of God's plan."[17] The 35 percent of Americans who as late as April 2021 believed "that Biden's victory was illegitimate" were disproportionately not only white, older, less educated, and Republican, but, according to credible surveys, "more religious (particularly Protestant and more likely to describe themselves as born again)."[18] These evangelicals got the message early and loud and clear from Pat Robertson. Two weeks after the election, Robertson told viewers of his 700 Club, "I think Trump's ultimately going to win." He added that "Satan" wanted Biden in office in order to "turn this nation over to socialism."[19]

To be sure, there are white evangelicals who ignore and even resist thinking of this kind. Often, these people connect their religion primarily to local communities and pay little attention to national politics. They would not see Josh Hawley as a mirror of themselves. Moreover, the ranks of white evangelicals have long included a vocal minority of economic and ethnoracial progressives. Since 1971, the magazine *Sojourners* has been a prominent forum for socially engaged evangelicals who reject Manichean assumptions and who try to engage their opponents in honest debate. There has long been a genuine "evangelical left."[20] But its marginality is illustrated by the career of Richard Cizik, who was removed in 2008 from his position as the Washington lobbyist for the National Association of Evangelicals because of his deviation from orthodox views on same-sex relationships and his heterodox prioritizing of environmental protection and economic equality.[21]

Cizik, like most of the people who tried to move evangelicalism in progressive directions, essentially copied elements of the ecumenical campaign for a more cosmopolitan Protestantism but did not admit it, certainly not in public. Each spiritual journey no doubt has its own integrity, but the development of progressive evangelicalism has been in large part a project in appropriation and effacement: the perspectives and programs of ecumenicals were appropriated for an "enriched" evangelicalism or a "post-evangelicalism," while the ecumenical sources of inspiration, so long scorned, were effectively effaced. A recent example of this syndrome is David P. Gushee, *After Evangelicalism: The Path to a New Christianity*, which vigorously endorses one traditional ecumenical idea after another while rarely identifying them as such.[22] Whatever value anyone might find in Gushee's "New Christianity," it is not new.

Far to Cizik's right, a good many evangelicals, Worthen observes, wanted heroes "who would stand up for their instincts about human nature, social order, and biblical law."[23] What millions of them turned out to really desire was what they got from adamantly Manichean Christian nationalists like Gary North: "We must use the doctrine of religious liberty to gain independence for Christian schools until we train up a generation of people who know that there is no religious neutrality, no neutral education, and no neutral civil government. Then they will get busy constructing a Bible-based social, political, and religious order which flatly denies the religious liberty of the enemies of God."[24]

The power of the Christian worldview was visible in the widely publicized 2021 letter from eleven members of Republican congressman Adam Kinzinger's family disowning him for voting to impeach Trump for high crimes and misdemeanors. The letter reveals how the evangelical faithful had been trained to think. Kinzinger's cousins treated his anti-Trump vote as tantamount to joining "the Devil's Army." The errant congressman had given up Christianity and gone against Trump, who really "is a Christian," supported by "Franklin Graham, Robert Jeffries," and other pastors who warrant that Trump is "a believer." Kinzinger should forsake the "false news" of the media and attend to Trump's "Christmas message," which "gave the plan of salvation, instructing people how to repent and ask the Savior into their heart to be 'Born Again!'" The family's letter voiced sadness that Kinzinger had "lost the respect of Lou Dobbs, Tucker Carlson, Sean Hannity, Laura Ingraham," and other Fox News personalities.[25] The operative standard for what it meant to be a good Christian was the approval of Fox's commentators.

Evangelical support for the unabashedly "immoral" Trump should not be treated as a mystery. That triumph fits with the culture of American evangelical Protestantism, the long-term history of which has been cogently summarized by historian John Fea:

> Evangelical fears that Barack Obama was a Muslim, and that as president he would violate the Second Amendment and take away their guns echo—and are about as well founded as—early American evangelicals' fear that Thomas Jefferson was going to seize believers' Bibles. The Christian Right's worries in the 1960s and 1970s that they might lose their segregated academies should take us back to the worries of white evangelicals who lived in the antebellum South. Contemporary efforts to declare America a Christian nation should remind us of similar attempts by fundamentalists a century ago. Efforts to portray immigrants—documented and undocumented—as threats to white Christian culture take us back to the days of evangelical support for the Know-Nothing Party.[26]

While the Republican Party's dependence on white voters who inherit this tradition was gradually becoming more pronounced, the Democratic Party was able to count on African

Americans, college graduates of all ethnicities, and voters who professed no religious affiliation.

Black voters, whose numbers increased exponentially after the Voting Rights Act of 1965, decisively abandoned the Party of Lincoln. From the mid-1960s onward, more than 80 percent of African American voters identified themselves with the Democratic Party and yet more voted for Democratic presidential candidates. As more African Americans were elected to state and federal offices, culminating after many decades in Barack Obama's presidential victories of 2008 and 2012, the relative importance of Blacks in the Democratic Party increased. The success of the Republicans in siphoning off white voters through the Southern Strategy created more space for African Americans. By 2016, nearly one-quarter of voters in Democratic Party primaries were Black. After Lyndon Johnson in 1964, no Democratic presidential candidate won a majority of white voters.

In 2020 the centrality of African Americans to the Democratic Party became obvious. By endorsing Joe Biden at a strategic time, Black congressional leader James Clyburn of South Carolina did more than any single individual to secure his party's presidential nomination for Biden. Without the benefit of African American politician Stacey Abrams's extraordinary grassroots mobilization programs, it is doubtful that Biden would have won Georgia's electoral votes or that Democrats would have won Georgia's two Senate seats. Moreover, without the overwhelming support of Black voters Biden would not have prevailed in the swing stages of Michigan, Pennsylvania, and Wisconsin. Kamala Harris's selection as Biden's vice presidential running mate surely owed something to her potential ability to appeal to African American voters. Not all African Americans are actively involved in Protestant churches, but the overwhelming majority share a church-intensive background. Hence the ethnoracial event of greater African American participation in public affairs is also an ethnoreligious event.

Catholics, too, became a more formidable political presence, marked initially by John F. Kennedy's election as president in 1960. Kennedy's election was part of a larger transformation then encouraged two years later by Vatican II, which freed American Catholics to accept religious pluralism and church-state separation. John Courtney Murray, the Jesuit thinker who advised Kennedy on his epochal speech vowing not to govern according to the dictates of Rome, facilitated this transformation of the Catholic outlook. Murray had struggled since the mid-1940s to persuade his superiors that Catholics would never exercise substantial influence in the United States unless they were willing to work within a constitutional system that did not confer special recognition to the Roman Catholic Church. After Vatican II, Catholics had an easier time getting elected or appointed to public office beyond the ethnic enclaves that had been their gateways into legislative and judicial power. By the early twenty-first century, Catholics constituted 20 percent of the national population, yet six of the nine US Supreme Court justices were Catholics, as were 30 percent of the members of the House of Representatives.[27]

Catholics helped Christianity retain its prominence in American society, but they did not become a dependable constituency for either political party. To be sure, from the 1930s through the 1960s the great majority of Catholic voters, especially working-class whites, were part of the Democratic Party's coalition. But as Catholics achieved upward social and economic mobility, they divided their votes between the two parties. In 1965, only 14 percent of the Catholic members of the House of Representatives were Republicans, but by 1997,

40 percent were. In 1965, all but two of the fourteen Catholic senators were Democrats, but in 2020 there were twenty-two Catholic senators, only twelve of whom were Democrats.

The Republican position on abortion influenced this drift to the right. Catholics who attended mass regularly were more likely to leave the Democrats when the Reagan-era Republicans identified abortion as a major issue. Yet more switched later, when the Republican efforts to expand "religious liberty" brought about an alliance with Catholic hospitals and social agencies that wanted to retain access to federal funding while refusing to provide reproductive health services as required by federal law. White Catholics were divided in their political affiliations. John Kerry, Nancy Pelosi, and Joe Biden were Catholics, but so, too, were some of the most conservative of Republican politicians, including Paul Ryan and Kevin McCarthy. Since 2000, a majority of white Catholics have voted for the Republican presidential candidate in every election. The growing population of Hispanic Catholics has usually voted for Democrats, but not always.

In the early twenty-first century, it was clear that the conservative political coalition around issues of gender, sexuality, and religious liberty reflected traditional Catholic teachings and depended on a substantial segment of Catholic voters as well as white evangelical Protestants. At the same time, the power of political views to overcome religious affiliations was shown by how little discussion there was regarding the election of a liberal Catholic as president in 2020. Sixty years before, when Kennedy was elected, the pope's proximity to Washington was seen as a real enough threat to be earnestly explained away. But the determination of the Republican Party to appoint Catholics to the US Supreme Court and elsewhere in the federal judiciary reflected a sound understanding of the Catholic political tradition. That tradition, diverse as it was, constituted a substantial resource to be drawn upon for conservative purposes.

The Democrats could rely on the rapidly growing population of religiously unaffiliated voters. These highly educated individuals are the least susceptible to QAnon fantasies. The numbers of self-identified nonreligious Americans began to increase in the 1980s, well after Catholic and ecumenical Protestant churches experienced sharp declines in membership. Until the early 1980s, only about 5 percent of Americans said "none" when asked to identify their religion, resulting in the popular practice of social scientists and journalists to speak of "nones" as a category. As late as 1990, well after the mainline denominations had lost large percentages of their members, only 8 percent gave that response, but a decade later the number had grown to 15 percent. By 2012, 20 percent of the population so described itself. In 2019, more than a quarter of the nation—26 percent— did so. The 2019 study, carried out by the Pew Research Center, found striking generational differences. Of persons born between 1981 and 1996, 40 percent reported no religion.[28] Pew found that by 2021, 29 percent of Americans had become "nones."[29]

Why did most of the people who, by leaving the churches, had created the statistical foundation for the "decline of the mainline" wait so long to tell pollsters what they had done? The answer is not clear, but going to church had long been socially approved behavior. Admitting that you were no longer doing it was more difficult for many Americans. By the early twenty-first century, however, post-Protestants and post-Catholics began to go on record about their lack of religious affiliation at accelerating speed. Once more than a handful were willing to say they had no religion—a tipping point?—it became easier for others. Even among African Americans, where church membership had always been high, nonaffiliation began to be reported much more often in the early twenty-first century.[30]

Former ecumenicals constituted the vast majority of the "nones." Recent membership figures posted by ecumenical denominations themselves leave no doubt about this. Between 2010 and 2018, the Disciples of Christ declined by 40 percent. The United Presbyterians lost 40 percent between 2009 and 2020. The Lutherans lost 22 percent between 2010 and 2019. The Dutch Reformed (Reformed Church in America) lost 45 percent between 2000 and 2020. The Episcopalians lost 29 percent between 2002 and 2019.[31] Post-Judaic Americans are certainly part of this group, but since less than 2 percent of the national population in the early twenty-first century is ethnically Jewish to begin with, post-Judaic Americans could constitute only a tiny fraction of the religiously unaffiliated. Some of nonaffiliates were ex-evangelicals. Progressive evangelical theologian David P. Gushee remarks that he knows of countless young people who got fed up with "inerrancy, indifference to the environment, deterministic Calvinism, purity culture, divine violence, Hallmark-Christmas-Movie Jesus, rejection of gay people, male dominance, racism, God = GOP, or whatever else."[32]

A substantial number of these nonaffiliates, however, had left the Roman Catholic Church, which lost members at about the same rate as the ecumenical Protestant churches. In their comprehensive study of church attendance, two sociologists conclude "that the key trend in attendance over the last half-century or more has been the decline in Catholic attendance to the level of that of mainline Protestants."[33] By 2020, more than one-third of the cradle Catholics in the United States no longer identified themselves as Catholic. The most thorough study of Catholic disaffiliation finds that about 17 percent of the Americans who have left the Catholic Church profess no religious affiliation—these are the "post-Catholics"—while 15 percent joined other Christian churches and 2 percent affiliate with non-Christian faiths. These figures include Hispanics. The traditional white demographic foundation of American Catholicism declined by about 40 percent in the past fifty years.[34]

Some Catholics found Vatican II's changes disappointing— too radical, or not radical enough. Others were uncomfortable remaining in an institution where the sexual abuse of children by priests seemed endemic and where women were excluded from the priesthood. The church's persistent opposition to contraception greatly diminished its authority for many women.[35] Other Catholics, like Protestants and religiously observant Jews, became indifferent to religion as they found other communities. Since churches and synagogues exist in part to serve needs for intimacy and belonging, their significance declined when people had easy access to alternative forms of community, including those made available by electronic communication networks. Moreover, as belief in hell and eternal punishment faded, churches lost some of the managerial authority they once exercised. Further, liberals had an additional incentive to declare their distance from any and all churches when the most widely quoted spokespersons for Christianity came to be those with a tolerance for white supremacy and expressed unabashedly reactionary views about sex and gender, including a hostility even to contraception.

Quite a few of the people who left the Protestant churches retained what historian Martin E. Marty calls a "Protestant deposit," a cultural layer that continued to affect how they processed their ongoing experience.[36] Some of the departing young people had been regular readers of the avant-garde youth magazine *motive*. William Stringfellow and Harvey Cox were contributors to this arts-and-culture periodical sponsored by the United Methodist Church. Conservative Methodists were outraged by its militant feminism, in defense of which church officials like Oxnam often faced down angry regional assemblies. But after many perceived provocations, the Methodists in 1969 ceased to finance the ecclesiastically troublesome operation. The editors responded by publishing, with their last remaining funds, what amounted to an institutional suicide bomb: two blockbuster issues celebrating same-sex relationships.

The career of one of *motive*'s editors, Charlotte Bunch, illustrates both the dynamics of exit from churches and the post-Protestant feeling of a connection to them. "When I came out as a lesbian in the context of the feminist movement," Bunch later wrote, "I was simply not willing to be affiliated with an institution that labeled me a sinner or denied me the right to enter its highest callings." Bunch was politicized by the multiracial youth conferences of her college years. She was elected president of the Methodists' national youth organization and then became a co-editor of *motive*. She left the Methodists, "impatient" with "the phallocentricity of Christianity and with the slowness of the institution to see how it oppressed women." Yet as a mature scholar and senior university professor, Bunch in 2003 testified to a feeling that her work "on feminism and human rights is still part of the struggle I began in the '60s to find a values-based politics that can give hope and vision for a better life for all."[37]

Just as the travels of the ecumenical elite enabled their churches to function for some as more capacious homes, for others these travels became stepping-stones to something different. Ecumenical Protestantism was often a way station on the road to post-Protestant secularism. Transitional spaces were vital for millions of American Protestants. The ecumenical churches created and sustained an environment in which it became more possible to engage sympathetically a vast panorama of ethnoracial, sexual, religious, and cultural varieties of humankind. These varieties threatened to destabilize inherited practices and beliefs, but the ecumenical churches provided a community and an orientation that facilitated these engagements for people who might have otherwise avoided them. That many millions continue to be at home in ecumenical churches does not render any less significant, historically, the transit-assisting function for other millions. Not everyone driven in the same direction by the same circumstances ends up in the same place.

Catholics dealt with the same needs somewhat differently. Because the Roman Catholic Church is institutionally monolithic, those who became post-Catholic experienced no strict equivalent to the ecumenical way station. These individuals found what transitional homes they could in liberal enclaves within Catholic churches, sometimes moving from one parish to another in search of more congenial company or transferring from a relatively conservative Catholic college to a more liberal one. But Catholic ecclesiastical structure encouraged an in-or-out framing for individual decisions. Liberal Catholics from Dorothy Day through Daniel Berrigan and Nancy Pelosi take positions at variance with papal decrees while strongly affirming Catholic identity. Those who identify themselves as "ex-Catholics," like most "ex-evangelicals," tend to be more critical of their natal communities than post-Protestants are of theirs.

Many ecumenical Protestants and many post-Protestants have much in common. This confluence is consistent with the easy back-and-forth between ecumenical Protestantism and secular liberalism going back several generations, well before church membership numbers diminished and post-Protestant numbers increased. Langdon Gilkey noted that ecumenical congregations even in the 1930s, 1940s, and 1950s were filled with "moderate, democratic, rationalistic, autonomous, tolerant" souls "almost indistinguishable" (except for a theism that could not even be taken for granted, Gilkey observed pointedly) from "the responsible, moral, humanistic, 'secular' culture around them." As other communities became available to these men and women, especially to their children, the move from churches "into a secular lifestyle represented a very small step, probably making a discernable difference only on Sunday mornings."[38]

Without the support of most of the post-Protestants and post-Catholics, the diversity-preoccupied public life of the United States of the late twentieth and early twenty-first centuries could not have come into being and the presidential victories of Barack Obama and Joe Biden would have been impossible. Not all of the "nones" had the same attitudes and values, but there is no doubt that the ethical orientation of many did reflect the teachings of their Congregationalist and Methodist tutors. Ecumenical leaders campaigned for "individualism, freedom, pluralism, tolerance, democracy, and intellectual inquiry," observes sociologist N. J. Demerath III, exactly the liberal values that gained ground in the last third of the twentieth century and were honored to some degree by most Americans outside of the Republican Party.[39]

These liberal values served as key justifications for many of the transformations of the 1960s and have been invoked since that time in countless specific contexts as the nation has confronted massive immigration from non-European lands and has sought to find ways to do justice to the descendants of its enslaved and conquered peoples. The liberal political theory of the former Episcopalian John Rawls is widely recognized as an example of post-Protestant thinking.[40] The long, stutter-step campaign of ecumenical Protestant leaders to achieve a more cosmopolitan Protestantism was not simply a product of internal self-reflection but also a product of engagement with the same modern social and cultural experiences that influenced secular contemporaries, including the demographic changes noted above. The campaign of the liberalizers did not follow from simply reading yet again the Sermon on the Mount, the book of James, and other scriptural foundations for liberalization. Science and worldly experience fueled the campaign, exactly as the modernists of the 1920s said they would.

Religious collectives, like other movements, are contingent entities, generated, sustained, transformed, diminished, and sometimes destroyed by the changing circumstances of history. But a survivalist bias has obscured recognition of the place of ecumenical Protestantism in these standard historical processes. A preference for if not a commitment to the survival of Christianity in general and of the institutions of Protestantism in particular can inhibit appreciation of the historic function of ecumenical Protestantism as a way station on the road to post-Protestant secularism. Most of the scholarly literature on ecumenical Protestantism has been written by survivalists disinclined to see departure from churches as anything other than declension. People with institutionalized responsibility for the flourishing of ecumenical churches are understandably slow to see post-Protestantism as anything other than a loss. Yet, only if one approaches history as a Christian survivalist is it invidious to recognize ecumenical Protestantism's historic role as a way station to something else. Was that "something else" really so bad? The question invites more sustained inquiry than the ecumenical intelligentsia has given it. Might ecumenical

Protestantism take some pride in facilitating post-Protestantism? The influence of ecumenical Protestantism on the public life of the United States will remain largely invisible if we look for it only in the churches.

But the churches did not disappear. Christianity was surviving. In what measure, in what form, and in service to what ends?

8

Christianity's American Fate

A CONSERVATIVE REFUGE?

Back out of all this now too much for us . . .
There is a house that is no more a house
Upon a farm that is no more a farm
And in a town that is no more a town. . . .
Your destination and your destiny's
A brook that was the water of the house,
Cold as a spring as yet so near its source,
Too lofty and original to rage. . . .
Here are your waters and your watering place.
Drink and be whole again beyond confusion.

—ROBERT FROST, 1947

IN 2012 THE BRITISH historian-philosopher Theo Hobson chided American ecumenicals for not taking every opportunity "to tell a strong story about the compatibility of Christianity and secular liberalism." This was "an immense failure," Hobson argued. "America can only be ideologically unified by this story."[1]

Whatever might or might not overcome the divisions among Americans, Hobson was certainly correct about the ideological disarray of American ecumenical intellectuals. Amid political polarization and secularization, ecumenical leaders struggled to maintain and clarify their Christian identity. If they were to serve as a "prophetic minority," as many suggested in the wake of their diminished size and standing, what were they to be prophetic about? Where in their program was the Bible, which the evangelicals claimed as theirs? How were they to make sense theologically, rather than just politically, of race, gender, and sexual orientation? Where were they allied with secularists, and where distant from them?

While attempting to engage these questions ecumenical leaders were obliged to deal with two unexpected and portentous developments. The first was the failure of the postwar merger movement. Plans for a unified, national Protestant church, so long in the making, came to nothing as early as the 1970s. Second was the growth of theologically and politically conservative churches in the Global South during the final decades of the twentieth century, changing the shape of what was recognized as Christianity. This transformation of the global Christian profile greatly strengthened the claims of American evangelicals that they—not the mainliners—were the true exemplars of the ancient faith. Ecumenicals had spent many decades urging American Christians to show more respect for the religious ideas and practices of peoples abroad, only to find those ideas and practices, as they matured, similar to those of their evangelical rivals at home.

Neither of these two developments has registered in popular and academic treatments of recent religious history.

The failure to fashion a single, national Protestant church was emotionally traumatic and theologically threatening. This crushing defeat came exactly at the historical moment when the ecumenical intelligentsia was taking the greatest risks in opposing imperialism abroad and racism at home and was beginning to notice a membership hemorrhage. By the early 1970s the governing bodies of nearly all denominations in the Consultation on Church Union had pulled out.[2] Most of the people who cared enough about churches to pay for their maintenance, often joined by their local pastors, sent a clear answer to the leadership. No!

Campaigners for a more cosmopolitan Protestantism were thus struck with the second installment of a historicist double whammy, the first of which had hit them in the mission field. Immersion in religious life abroad made it impossible to ignore the historical particularity of American denominations. Now, the anti-sectarian follow-up at home, designed to act on the lessons learned abroad, revealed that traditional rituals, doctrines, and tribal identities really mattered. Historical particularity was not a pathology, to be overcome therapeutically, but was essential to what churches actually were. That individuals would "lose an essential locus of identity in already depersonalized society" was the most common concern of critics of the merger movement.[3]

Was the notion of a transhistorical gospel a fantasy? This fear had hovered like a ghost above ecumenical apologetics, decade after decade. H. Richard Niebuhr himself fled from it early on, shortly after he had documented the depth and power of particularism in his *Social Sources of Denominationalism*. Eight years later, in 1937, he answered himself with *The Kingdom of God in America*, arguing that American Protestantism had been united by an expectation that God's kingdom would actually come about on earth, eventually. There was some basis for this claim about what American Protestants thought, but it was a thin foundation for any hope that denominational divisions could ever be overcome. Earnestly, Niebuhr called on the faithful to renew their "reliance on the divine initiative," thereby to "infuse new life" into American Protestantism.[4] But Niebuhr's empirical findings about the dynamics of disunity endured, while his call for renewed commitment faded into the generalized hope of his generation's seminarians.

The globally engaged leadership, having ventured far ahead of its constituency in dismissing particularistic identities as retrograde, was embarrassed. If its churches were to be salvaged, the cosmopolitan campaigners were obliged to chart earthly paths that the faithful and their local ministers might actually walk. Outlining that future was made more difficult by an ironic fact: the role of denominations in the Christian project did decline, but not as expected. Megachurches took up more and more organizational space in American Protestantism after the 1970s. These huge enterprises, often near Walmart or Target box stores in the bourgeoning suburban and exurban shopping malls, bore almost no resemblance to what denominationalism's ecumenical critics hoped to see. Entrepreneurially skilled, charismatic preachers, proclaiming a simple, evangelical gospel, built followings in the thousands and even tens of thousands, eventually growing to millions through television and social media. Most had little or no connection to any larger ecclesiastical body, although some of the leading televangelists of the late twentieth century, including Pat Robertson, were affiliated with the Southern Baptist Convention. Robertson's *700 Club*, begun in 1966, eventually broadcast in dozens of languages and claimed an annual audience of 360 million people throughout the globe.

Hence the ecumenical leadership, having experienced the failure of its own plans for a large, integrated American church working in tandem with the World Council of Churches and other ecumenical institutions throughout the world, found it-self watching evangelicals succeed in building national and global followings of prodigious size and wealth. Meanwhile, their own local congregations in small towns and urban neighborhoods were struggling. Proud of their large, imposing edifices with tall steeples, typically built between 1890 and 1940, the Presbyterians were on one downtown corner, the Methodists on another, and the Episcopalians just a block or two away. But the members of these congregations were graying and the churches were losing many of their children. By the end of the twentieth century many merged with neighboring churches of kindred denominations to avoid becoming too small to afford a full-time minister. For pas-toral leadership, the smallest congregations came to rely on part-timers with only the brief apprentice-like training offered by "academies" that functioned as alternatives to seminaries. From a theological point of view, it was rather like substituting a bar review course for three years of law school, but it kept the churches alive. In many American downtowns, the capacious church build-ings of the old "Protestant establishment" were sold to flourishing Pentecostal congregations.

Amid these unwelcome circumstances, seminaries and di-vinity schools understood it was part of their responsibility to figure out what should be done.[5] Where was the campaign for a more cosmopolitan Protestantism to go? In the halls of these institutions the notion of ecumenical Protestantism as a "pro-phetic minority" took its most vibrant shape, deeply responsive to the progressive movements in the surrounding society.

Just which issues mattered most? Concerns about economic inequality lost much of their earlier hold on ecumenical atten-tion. The Social Gospel as developed by Washington Gladden, Walter Rauschenbusch, and Jane Addams had prioritized economic justice. This tradition was renewed in the 1940s heyday of ecumenical Protestantism. Then, after being soft pedaled in the face of McCarthy Era red-baiting, calls to end economic inequality returned with a vengeance in the early 1960s in the manifestos of the Stringfellow-Cox generation. But this priority did not last. Amid the multicultural enthusiasm of the later twentieth century, the identity politics prominent in the nation's liberal left played out noisily in the ecumenical churches, just as it did in higher education and in the Democratic Party. The universalist ideology that had been a defining feature of ecumenical Protestantism, and that served as a justification for its progressive engagements of the 1940s, 1950s, and 1960s, fell under deep suspicion, often accused—with some justice—of serving as a cover for white male privilege. Programs that were not significantly defined by ethnoracial or sex- and gender-related identity groups lost purchase. What did survive, and became one of the chief triumphs of the campaign for a more cosmopolitan Protestantism, was the antiracist legacy of the Stringfellow-Cox generation.

Liberation Theology changed the terms of academic debates about Christianity. This international movement had strong proponents in Catholic Spain and Latin America but in American Protestantism was led by James Cone. His early books, *Black Theology and Black Power* (1969) and *A Theology of Black Liberation* (1970), vilified white theologians for not addressing anti-Black racism and established Cone as an intellectual and political powerhouse at Union Theological Seminary in New York City. In this early phase of his career, Cone argued that Christ was himself virtually Black, and an agent of Black liberation, worldwide. Eschewing theology's traditional claims to universality, Cone insisted on radical particularism. "As a Black theologian, I want to know what God's revelation means right now as the Black community participates in the struggle for liberation. *Revelation is a Black event*—it is what Blacks are doing about their liberation." In later years, Cone became more welcoming of the markedly different understanding of Christianity advanced by Martin Luther King Jr., and indeed by most African American religious and political leaders. In *Martin & Malcolm & America,* a book published in 1991, Cone held that the reconciliation perspective of King and the militantly separatist perspective of Malcolm X corrected and complemented each other.[6]

Theological leadership in the ecumenical seminaries and divinity schools increasingly passed into the hands of African Americans like Cone and white feminists like Catherine Keller.[7] African American transgender feminist Pauli Murray, who had been a cofounder of the National Organization of Women in 1966, became an Episcopal priest in 1977.[8] But the gains of feminism and Black liberation were mitigated by the fact that theology itself was no longer as important in national conversations as it once had been. In a great historical irony, just when ecumenical theology became a setting for exceptional creativity by African Americans and women, theology itself was rapidly losing standing in the public culture of the nation.

While Cone underestimated the antiracist politics of his predecessors, his representation of theology as practiced in American seminaries during the previous several decades was not inaccurate. With the exception of Princeton Theological Seminary's Richard Shaull, the leading white professors of theology even in the 1960s did not address race theologically with the directness that Cone did. For all their progressive politics, their theology remained dominated by themes developed in nineteenth- and early twentieth-century Germany.[9] The theology taught in the ecumenical seminaries, observed Gary Dorrien, had become "too secular for religious believers, too religious for secularists, and too academic for non-theologians."[10]

In 2003 Keller offered an unusually candid summary of how theology had tumbled "off the line of progress": "[Theology] partakes little of the optimistic gleam of scientific progress, the insouciant originality of the arts. When for the sake of that sparkling novelty or that cultured public, religious thinkers dwell on the 'cutting edge,' they lose their traditional constituencies— and *ipso facto*, ironically, the activist potential that distinguishes progressive theology. Inasmuch, however, as we honor the constitutive accountability of, say, Christian theology to the church, we cannot escape the dogmatic drag, the vortex of swirling symbols and insecure institutions."[11] Here, Keller alludes to the tension between the impulse to innovate in response to new conditions and the need to honor the sentiments of the members of the community of faith. The entire history of the campaign for a more cosmopolitan Protestantism was a struggle to resolve this tension. Keller's own response to this "double bind," Dorrien explained, was to pitch theology "to environmentalists, radical feminists, liberation movements, and antiglobalization activists."[12]

But did people involved in those movements need theology? The secular movements Dorrien named were among those that had attracted young people, especially into the ranks of post-Protestants and post-Catholics. Cone's theology drew heavily from the secular Black Power movement, many of whose leaders displayed little interest in churches. The most visible of the feminist theologians of that generation, the Catholic Mary Daly, eventually abandoned the church altogether.[13] Theology had always drawn some of its content from the surrounding culture, and theology's mission was often understood to include dialogue with the world in which churches found themselves. But just what was Christianity contributing to that dialogue? Dorrien noted that academic theology "became more liberationist, feminist, environmentalist, multiculturalist, and postmodernist" while "the churches to which the liberal theologians belonged" accepted only mild forms of feminism and environmentalism while "battling annually over gay rights" and swinging toward "great homogeneity and confessional identity."[14]

"Battling over gay rights" was indeed a major locus of the clash between American ecumenical and evangelical Protestants, and among ecumenicals themselves, during the last decades of the twentieth century and the early decades of the twenty-first. For evangelicals, the battle was mostly against outsiders, but ecumenicals at every institutional level, from local congregations through regional assemblies to denominational governance, divided passionately over the status of LGBTQ parishioners, sanctioning same-sex marriages, and the ordination of gay and lesbian clergy. This was true across the color line: Blacks, whose influence within the ecumenical leadership increased during these same years, joined many white Protestants in resisting liberal social and legal perspectives on LGBTQ issues. Heather R. White and other scholars have shown that the opposition to same-sex intimacy was in fact a minor theme in the Christian tradition across the centuries. But evangelicals brought it into greater prominence. Ecumenicals found the debate impossible to avoid.[15]

It was exactly while debating LGBTQ issues that ecumenical churches were obliged to deal with the second of the unexpected, portentous developments that complicated the challenges of ecumenical leadership following the "decline of the mainline."

Christians in the Global South, soon constituting a majority of the world's professing Christians, had strong opinions about same-sex relationships. The faith that caught on and flourished in most of Africa and much of Asia and Latin America took directions the ecumenical missionaries had discouraged as anachronistic and lacking in spiritual maturity. The evangelical missionaries who dominated the mission fields after the departure of their ecumenical counterparts often encouraged Global South Christianity's vigorous opposition to same-sex intimacy by supporting indigenous leaders who were responsive to that message. Paul's apparent approval of the death sentence for homosexual intercourse in Romans 1:27–32 had more credibility in Uganda than it did in all but the most extreme of American congregations.[16]

Some American denominations were able to treat Global South Christianity as a thing apart, but governance arrangements made this impossible for Methodists, Episcopalians, and several other groups. Delegates from Africa, Asia, and Latin America were empowered to participate in policy making. Repeatedly, these representatives joined with US-based conservatives in voting down anti-homophobic resolutions when brought to denominational assemblies.

The theological imperative to welcome all believers into the Body of Christ meant that Global South Christianity was another example of demographic diversification by long distance, but with new and ironic consequences. Earlier episodes had challenged conservatives and inspired liberals, but the egalitarian imperative to welcome Global South Christians into full fellowship now had exactly the opposite result. It provided new allies to American evangelicals. Ecumenicals had spent decades demanding more deference to "indigenous" Christians, as the convert communities in missionary-targeted societies were called. "We" need to listen to "them" and should not tell them exactly how to be a Christian. Okay, here "they" were.

A Kenyan bishop blessed Sarah Palin in her own Assembly of God church in 2008, praying that the Republican Party's vice presidential candidate would be safe from witches. Was it racist to find this objectionable? Was it patronizing to let it pass and to refrain from criticizing it? How much of American Protestant progressivism was actually a form of colonialism, a continuation of Western arrogance? A Nigerian bishop tried to perform a rite of exorcism on a gay British priest at a meeting of the global Anglican Communion. An American bishop criticized this act and was forced to apologize.[17]

Global South Christianity became problematic for the Americans and Europeans not only as extensively homophobic but as lacking in support for the ideal of gender equality—a value that since the 1960s had become an important part of ecumenical Protestantism in the United States. Even evangelical confessions that had embraced some forms of gender equality experienced adamant opposition from coreligionists in the Global South. The Seventh-day Adventists, an evangelical denomination that originated in the United States in the 1860s, were unable to ordain women year after year because delegates from Africa, Latin America, and Asia (almost 90 percent of Adventists lived outside North America by 2010) kept voting down measures calling for women's ordination. Paul the Apostle explicitly prohibited it in 1 Corinthians 14:34–35: "The women should keep silent in the churches. For they are not permitted to speak, but should be in submission. . . . If they desire to learn anything, let them ask their own husbands at home; for it is improper for a woman to speak in church."[18] Selected scriptures were interpreted more literally than most American Christians, including many evangelicals, could easily welcome. Rwandan bishops justified genocide by citing Samson's slaughter of Philistines.[19]

Not all varieties of religion practiced in the Global South under the sign of Christianity were in significant tension with practices in the ecumenical churches of North America and Western Europe. Denominational and transdenominational organizations maintained cordial, collegial relationships with some of the "new" churches. Institutes and programs devoted to "Global Christianity" have replaced "foreign missions," an encouraged, sustained, reciprocal contact.[20]

Yet more than enough of Global South Christianity differed from American ecumenical norms to make the question of the borders of the faith inescapable. Did Christianity have no boundaries, other than the self-professions of individuals? The history of the faith was filled with quarrels about its boundaries, with parties accusing one another of not being "real" Christians. The spectacular rise of Global South churches brought this old question to the fore, yet again, and with unprecedented force. Who is to say that the growing churches of Tanzania and Brazil are not as Christian as the Southern Baptists of Texas, or the Episcopalians of San Francisco, or the Catholics of Boston?

Some observers toyed with the theologically dangerous question, as expressed by Brian Stanley, "whether Christianity has converted indigenous religions or whether indigenous religions and cultural perspectives . . . have succeeded in converting Christianity." Stanley raised this question about some "white North American" as well as "African, Asian, [and] Latin American" practices claiming to be Christian, but the Global South presented a more formidable challenge than the American "prosperity gospel" to the notion that Christianity had a clear and singular essence.[21]

A popular means of recognizing the Christianity of the Global South while establishing some critical distance from it was the representation of Global South Christianity as a "third church," like Catholicism and Protestantism, comparable but different. Historian Philip Jenkins is an influential defender of this approach. Perhaps, Jenkins observes, "only in the newer churches" can the Bible "be read with any authenticity and immediacy." Perhaps "the Old Christendom should listen attentively to Southern voices." In the eyes of "the poor and persecuted" in many areas of the globe, Jenkins suggested to his Western readers, "the book of Revelation looks like true prophecy on an epic scale," and the notion of "the government as Antichrist is not a bizarre religious fantasy but a convincing piece of political analysis."[22] Indeed, it served the interests of the most conservative of American Protestants to downplay the differences.

This reluctance to emphasize differences is true of many evangelical visitors to Africa. Melani McAlister shows that American evangelicals who return home from mission-driven visits to Africa often rhapsodize about the apparent authenticity of the faith they witnessed. They are "enchanted" with what they take to be the simple purity of mind and spirit they find in African worship services, reminiscent, they think, of the raw passion of the earliest churches as described in the New Testament. These visitors usually screen out the economic, social, and political complexities of the lives of the local Christians. The American tourists McAlister studied were quick, however, to recognize Muslim persecution of African Christians, which they connected to what they alleged was secular persecution of Christians in the United States. McAlister finds that American evangelical engagement with the Global South intensified an evangelical self-conception as "victims."[23] Evangelicals tell pollsters that they, much more than Muslims, are the real victims of prejudice in the United States.

Thus the "global perspective" championed by the cosmopolitan elites of American Protestantism came to imply an

obligation to respect, rather than challenge, the most conservative of American theological and cultural attitudes. Solidarity
with the Christians of the Global South ended up enhancing
evangelical claims to speak for Christianity. The larger the presence of Christianity in the world, the more weight was carried
by anyone holding the franchise in any particular, national setting. By the early years of the twenty-first century, most of the
world's Christians lived outside the United States and Europe,
and a majority were Pentecostals. Membership numbers were
wielded like clubs against anyone suggesting that the world was
experiencing secularization. Christianity was stronger than
ever, and it was increasingly evangelical. Even more of Christianity's symbolic capital fell into the hands of evangelicals.[24]

As evangelical voices became louder in the United States,
bolstered by the size of theologically congenial Global South
Christianity, it became increasingly difficult for ecumenicals to
be heard in national arenas. While stories about religion in the
popular press were occasionally about Catholics and religiously
observant Jews, and sometimes about Muslims, more often
than not they were about white evangelicals. Journalists seemed
never to tire of interviewing Oklahoma preachers, Southern
Baptist seminary presidents, and random habitués of small-
town diners in "middle America." Ralph Sockman was the last
ecumenical preacher to command a national audience, yet by
the end of the 1950s even he had been eclipsed by Billy Graham.
The great North Carolina evangelist enjoyed the attention of the
media and the ear of many presidents, especially Nixon, Ford,
Reagan, and both Bushes. Even William Barber II, among the
most famous of today's African American ecumenical leaders,
has never approached the media prominence of his white evangelical counterparts, including Richard Land of the Southern
Baptist Convention.[25] Early in 2022, *New York Times* columnist

David Brooks made no reference to ecumenical Protestants in an ambitious account of the progressive elements of American evangelicalism and their potential to lead a "renewal" of Christianity, despite the decades-long espousal by ecumenicals of the more enlightened faith Brooks admired.[26]

Only with the election of Raphael Warnock to the US Senate in 2020 did an ecumenical preacher or theologian again become a household word in the United States. Warnock was the pastor of what had been the congregation of Martin Luther King Jr. in Atlanta, but, beyond that, was a student of theologian James Cone and himself a contributor to Liberation Theology. Like King, Warnock was resolutely in the ecumenical tradition. He acknowledged the educational and theological divide within African American churches. His religious outlook was transformed by Morehouse College. "My parents were very, very conservative evangelicals," Warnock told the *New York Times* in 2021. But at Morehouse he "moved from a tradition that emphasized prayer and personal salvation to one that took a more activist approach."[27] He then studied at the liberal Protestant intellectual bastion Union Theological Seminary. Warnock's chief public identity is now as an elected politician, but he is also an emblem for the increased role of Blacks in leading the ecumenical Protestantism that was, itself, becoming a smaller part of American public life.

Were there other Warnocks in the religious pipeline? Not many. The drift to post-Protestantism during the half century between 1970 and 2020 decimated the potential leadership of ecumenical Protestantism. The seminaries had trouble recruiting ministerial students. Able men and women, Black and white, who might have entered the ministry as late as the 1960s were not interested. Those who wanted to engage contemporary intellectual movements, including those responsive to the traditions of Christianity, could easily find secular academic programs for which the seminaries were usually poor substitutes, often playing catch-up or taking this or that methodological or ideological movement to a curious extreme. University professors of philosophy, history, literature, sociology, and anthropology were inclined to dismiss seminaries as academia's hospices, where ideas went to die.

The seminaries themselves were literally dying. Many closed or moved in with still-healthy relatives. In the early twenty-first century, Andover-Newton, Bangor, Crozier, Episcopal Divinity, Pacific Lutheran, San Francisco, Southern California, and Trinity Lutheran closed or merged with other seminaries or were folded into universities. The institutions best able to survive were divinity schools affiliated from the start with major universities, including Harvard, Boston, Yale, Chicago, Emory, Duke, Southern Methodist, and Vanderbilt. A connection to functioning, all-purpose universities made a difference both intellectually and institutionally. A seminary was obliged to make it alone, but a divinity school could strengthen its ties to academic departments in relevant fields and draw support from a campus administration. Meanwhile, on the other side of the ecumenical-evangelical divide, free-standing seminaries continued to flourish, including Fuller, Gordon-Conwell, and Southern Baptist.

Academic departments of religion and religious studies were once thought to provide alternatives to seminaries and divinity schools as settings for scholarship and teaching unbound from the confessional commitments appropriate for a church-related institution. These programs proliferated in the 1960s especially in private, but also in public universities, usually trying to do justice to the full panorama of classical world religions, in addition to Christianity. Often, they developed highly sophisticated programs in subfields like Buddhist Studies, Judaic Studies, and Islamic Studies. Invariably interdisciplinary, units of religious studies included anthropologists, historians, sociologists, and literary scholars. Religious Studies programs became caught up in theoretical debates about the applicability of the very concept of "religion": does it really refer to something distinctive and universal in culture and history or to just a collection of quite disparate phenomena so embedded in their contexts as to make comparison and generalization impossible? Did all of the "world's great religions"—not to mention the many so-called new religions—share enough elements to justify their study under that rubric? Moreover, if the very concept of "religion" as applied beyond the historically Christian North Atlantic West was a "colonialist move," as was often alleged, weren't scholars of Religious Studies complicit in furthering cultural hegemony?

Religious Studies departments and programs did advance cosmopolitan outlooks. They were largely founded by ecumenical Protestant scholars but were increasingly dominated by post-Protestants, some of whom bore an animus toward Christianity and the West. These programs often occupied a limbo between faith-affirming communities and institutions on one hand and the established disciplines that continued to study, within their own evolving portfolios, the phenomena conventionally classified as "religious" but without the institutional imperative to declare what that meant on the other. After all, anyone could study Confucianism or Daoism without worrying whether or not it was a religion. Only Religious Studies specialists were obliged to ponder that.

As theology declined except as a theoretical foundation for social activism, the chief topics of public debate across the ecumenical-evangelical divide became racism, sexism, and homophobia, and it was a debate characterized by the striking absence of what once been a core feature of traditional Protestantism: biblical hermeneutics. This meant that ecumenical voices in the public arena were mostly silent about the one cluster of fundamental issues on which they might have spoken with unique authority and sophistication: what the Bible actually was, how it should be read, and how it could guide conduct in today's society. Anyone can debate sexism and racism and homophobia. But the seminary elite was trained in the study of the Bible. And Protestantism was, after all, preeminently a textual religion. *Sola scriptura*, the Reformation fathers had proclaimed. Although these ecumenical intellectuals did cite scriptural passages in support of progressive causes and disputed evangelical interpretations of Romans 1:27–32 on same-sex intimacy, they rarely went beyond this piecemeal criticism to explain why their own perspective on the Bible was superior to that of their evangelical counterparts.

Might ecumenical intellectuals have more openly and clearly proclaimed that the Bible is a literary document containing profound and instructive passages that, when integrated with modern social and intellectual experience, can serve as a cultural anchor, a foundation for community, and a source of ethical inspiration? This conception of the Bible had long been readily available in the writings of liberal theologians. Even the doctrine of atonement—that "Christ died for our sins," as Paul phrased it in 1 Corinthians 15:3—is best read, argued Martin Luther King Jr.'s mentor, L. Harold DeWolf, as a holdover from the ancient practice of blood sacrifice. "The description of Christ as a substitute for the bloody sacrificial offerings of old," DeWolf explained in 1953, "now seems at best a quaint and alien figure of speech having no real interpretive value, while at worst it seems to imply acceptance of superstitious and unworthy notions."[28]

The Bible was easily appreciated as a moving record of the formation of the Christian project in the context of the traditions of the ancient Hebrews. Recognition of its historicity united secular admirers of the Bible with liberal Christians. Accurate history had not disqualified the Bible for use in many Christian communities. Indeed, ecumenical pastors routinely encouraged their congregations to appreciate the Bible for its stories, rather than for its doctrines. Harvey Cox was at his least controversial when he observed that "a historical-critical view of the Bible has deepened, not destroyed, our respect for its truth."[29]

"The function of the New Testament stories," Van A. Harvey argued in 1996, tracking Rudolf Bultmann, is not to "assent to supernatural claims." Rather, the point is "to provide a rich series of narratives that the members of the Christian community can use to reflect on their lives." There is no need to regard the gospels or the letters of Paul as recording actual historical events, Harvey continued; rather, the scriptures "provide pictures and imagery on which the imagination, so to speak, can dwell and that can be the basis for a call to a renewal of one's life."[30]

Yet in the public sphere increasingly dominated by evangelical voices, the ecumenical intelligentsia made little effort to plant their own flag in the Bible. This decision to hold back is one of the most remarkable choices made in the entire history of the campaign for a more cosmopolitan Protestantism. Langdon Gilkey took his ecumenical colleagues to task in the mid-1990s for this "conspiracy of silence."[31] This reluctance to engage in Bible talk had its advantages. One could thereby avoid overt clashes within the community of faith. More important, perhaps, one could avoid the risk that some parishioners, upon learning what the preachers really thought about the Bible, might be more inclined to depart. But political peace and intellectual passivity had real costs. Ecumenical reluctance to publicly proclaim their view of the Bible facilitated the transferal of Christianity's symbolic capital into the hands of evangelicals, who were glad to claim it. The Bible belonged to them, more than ever.

Episcopal bishop John Shelby Spong was an exception to the avoidance of sustained, public argumentation about biblical hermeneutics. But Spong was regularly patronized by academic theologians as a pretentious iconoclast. Spong suggested that the Apostle Paul was a repressed homosexual and that Jesus of Nazareth had been married to Mary Magdalene. Spong scorned evangelicals for taking seriously the idea of the virgin birth of Jesus. Ministers and church officials often warned the faithful that Spong was too far out to be part of the ecumenical mainstream.[32] For evangelicals, he was simply wild and not a real interlocutor. A more recent—and much more cautious— exception to the avoidance of detailed argumentation about the Bible is Tony Keddie's *Republican Jesus: How the Right Has Rewritten the Gospels*, which documents the link between evangelical hermeneutics and the policies of the Republican Party.[33]

Ecumenical intellectuals proved to be more comfortable attacking the "New Atheists" than taking evangelicals to task for a flawed interpretation of the Bible. Sam Harris, the most popular of the freethinking writers of the early twenty-first century to whom journalists applied that label, complained in 2005 that "moderates," as he called them, "did not permit anything very critical to be said about religious literalism." Harris and the other New Atheists made little effort to understand nonfundamentalist Christianity and rarely acknowledged the function of churches in building and maintaining communities. They focused almost entirely on the content of belief. But Harris and

his cobelligerents were correct to ascribe to ecumenical Protestants a high degree of tolerance for biblical interpretations they
knew to be intellectually indefensible. Harris was also correct
to insist that "moderate" versions of Christianity were the result
of "two thousand years of human thought" and a process of
education by which knowledge of nature, society, and history
was disseminated.[34]

Christian apologists of many orientations criticized Harris,
Richard Dawkins, and other New Atheists for their ostensibly
unsophisticated criticisms of religion. Yet this ritualized dis-
missal of the New Atheists almost always elided a very important fact. Vast numbers of the faithful espoused the crude ideas
the New Atheists attacked. "To dismiss atheist critiques as substituting caricatures for finely shaded portraits," complained
philosopher Philip Kitcher, "overlooks the obvious fact that,
however subtle the religious conceptions of those who inhabit
divinity schools or faculties of religion ... many believers
would acquiesce in the interpretive approaches assumed by the
critics, reading religious doctrines exactly as they do."[35] The
New Atheists may have been wrong about religion in general,
but they were more right than wrong about specific religious
ideas that were widely accepted in the United States. Rather
than welcoming the New Atheists as imperfect allies, most ecumenical intellectuals dismissed them, circling the wagons of the
community of faith.

At the beginning of the third decade of the twenty-first
century, the nation's most widely respected defender of the
spiritual traditions of ecumenical Protestantism is arguably not
a theologian or a preacher or a biblical scholar but the novelist
Marilynne Robinson. Her four "Gilead novels," centering on
the small-town Iowa lives of Congregationalists and Presbyterians in the 1950s, constitute a singular event in American

religious history. The chief characters in *Gilead, Home, Lila,* and *Jack* display plenty of frailty as well as wisdom and courage. Robinson's portrait of the Congregationalist pastor John Ames is one of the most sensitive explorations of ministerial subjectivity ever written. But her picture of what is perhaps the finest in American Protestantism is locked in the past. Robinson's nonfiction essays tried to perform contemporary philosophy and theology yet do not earn their conclusions because she begs countless questions that theorists are expected to answer. These essays, moreover, are persistently limited in their intellectual inventory. One of her sketches of American history identifying thinkers who might serve as resources for charting the nation's future mentions only Congregationalists.[36] Robinson's readership is wide, and her skills as a novelist are extraordinary. But the ecumenical Protestantism she champions is most powerful when out of apparent reach. The religious witness she performs can be universally welcomed because it serves primarily as a museum.

By the time Robinson gained popularity as a spokesperson for ecumenical Protestantism, the Christian project's relation to the nation was quite different from what it had been for nearly all of American history. As the secularization process reduced the size of Christianity in the United States, white evangelicals who believed they had a proprietary claim on the nation dominated Christianity's hollowed-out remnant.

Had Christianity become a refuge for white Protestants and Catholics on the conservative side of the salient political, cultural, and theological spectra? Yes, more than ever. But not exclusively. Renegade white evangelicals like Jim Wallis, Beth Moore, and David Gushee insisted that an evangelical orientation need not mean conservative politics. The diminished ecumenical Protestant and liberal Catholic populations still existed, often invoking scriptural inspiration for left-liberal public policy. The National Council of Churches continued its traditional role as a progressive lobby.

But the most striking challenge to conservative control of the franchise was the vitality of African American Protestantism. Black churchgoers, heirs to a distinctive tradition in which churches were the only institutions Black people were able to operate on their own, did not depart Christianity nearly as rapidly as whites.[37] Christianity remained a substantial locus of community and a foundation for social action. In 2021, 66 percent of African Americans identified themselves as Protestant and 6 percent as Catholic, and another 3 percent were Jehovah's Witnesses and other smaller confessions. In that year, slightly less than half of the American population as a whole belonged to any Christian church at all. The majority of African American Protestants were affiliated with either one of the historically Black denominations associated with the National Council of Churches or with one or another of the "mainline" denominations.

Even those African Americans whose theological opinions could be credibly classified as evangelical according to the "quadrilateral" are not typically allied with white evangelicals in public affairs. The common observation that American evangelicalism includes Blacks may be doctrinally true, but otherwise trivial and misleading. African Americans, even with relatively low levels of formal education, have had a worldly education in American social practices that inoculated them against many of the ideas white evangelicals found compatible with evangelically flavored theologies. "On nearly every social and political issue," Du Mez correctly summarizes the relevant studies, "black Protestants apply their faith in ways that run counter to white evangelicalism."[38]

Yet the total numbers of politically nonconservative Christians of any and all ethnoracial groups continue to dwindle. Even if nearly three-quarters of American Blacks identify as Christians, African Americans constitute only about 12 percent of the national population. Relative Black loyalty to the faith is not enough to alter the trend. Secularization, so long denied, is accelerating.[39] Secularization "may not be inevitable," the dean of the Harvard Divinity School concluded in 2020, but is "likely to be irreversible . . . except in relatively minor and temporary ways."[40]

If nonconservatives want to advance their own versions of Christianity within the American national frame, instead of being content to nourish the spiritual health of a particular silo of believers, they increasingly depend on allies outside the community of faith, especially the post-Protestants and post-Catholics who constitute most of the nonreligious population.

Brian Stanley has correctly described the decisions of the ecumenical leadership as decisive in yielding to evangelicals the upper hand in representing what was recognized in the United States as Christianity: "The mainline denominations estimated the prevailing sentiment to be one of radical humanism and commitment to human rights, whereas the conservatives judged the public preference to be for free market forms of highly individualized programs for self-betterment. . . . The liberals got it wrong and the conservatives got it right."[41]

The conservatives got it "right" in the competition for control of the Christian franchise in the United States. Doubling down on a business-friendly individualism and turning away from human rights was a highly effective means of achieving that goal. But what if the goal was larger? What if the choices the two groups made were to be assessed in a world-historical context, understanding Christianity not as an end in itself but as a historically particular vehicle for values that transcend it? Might wisdom then belong to those who looked beyond the immediate control of the Christian project? Might that project be an "earthen vessel," a worldly instrument?[42]

If we take this instrumental view of Christianity, there is no cause to lament its American fate as in part to serve as a way station to something beyond Christianity. But the remainder of that fate depends heavily on who controls what is left of it.

9

Beyond the Paradox of a Religious Politics in a Secular Society

What is divinity if it can come
Only in silent shadows and in dreams?
Shall she not find in comforts of the sun,
In pungent fruit and bright, green wings, or else
In any balm or beauty of the earth,
Things to be cherished like the thought of heaven?
Divinity must live within herself:
Passions of rain, or moods in falling snow;
Grievings in loneliness, or unsubdued
Elations when the forest blooms; gusty
Emotions on wet roads on autumn nights;
All pleasures and all pains, remembering
The bough of summer and the winter branch.
These are the measures destined for her soul.

—WALLACE STEVENS, 1915

THE UNITED STATES confronts a remarkable paradox: an *increasingly secular society is saddled with an increasingly religious politics*. In 2021, 29 percent of the national population identified as having no religious affiliation, but only 0.2 percent of members of Congress did.[1] Federal courts, dominated by Republican-appointed judges, have expanded the meaning of the "free exercise" clause of the First Amendment while limiting the scope of that amendment's prohibition on the establishment of religion. The courts have granted exemptions based on "sincerely held" claims of conscience that allow individuals and groups to discriminate against LGBTQ Americans or deny women access to reproductive health services.

The democratic process was not compromised when the "conscience exemption" was developed in 1940 to enable individual members of tiny pacifist sects to avoid military conscription.[2] But that process is threatened when "religious liberty" becomes a means for large populations to escape the reach of federal and state laws. The conscience exception has been expanded drastically to confer privilege on ideas professed by millions of citizens, and even by multimillion-dollar corporations.[3] In *Burwell v. Hobby Lobby Stores, Inc.*, the US Supreme Court in 2014 ruled that the mandate in the Patient Protection and Affordable Care Act requiring companies to pay for contraceptive services for their employees violated a privately held, for-profit corporation's right to religious freedom.[4] In *Fulton v. City of Philadelphia* (2021) the court ruled that Philadelphia violated the free exercise clause by failing to give Catholic Social Services an exemption from the nondiscrimination provisions in the city's public service contracts that would require CSS to screen prospective foster parents without regard to their sexual orientation or marital status.[5]

Dealing with the paradox of an increasingly religious politics in an increasingly secular society is made more difficult by the practice of protecting religious ideas from critical scrutiny. This informal ban on "the questioning of someone about their religion," laments Linda Greenhouse, is the "last taboo in American society." This ban "has been a gift to the religious right: the secular middle does not know how to talk back or even how to frame the questions."[6] The fear that one will be accused of being "biased against religion" has enabled conservative Christianity to exercise disproportionate influence over the public affairs of the United States, pushing aside liberal versions of Christianity and other perspectives, including secularism.[7]

The notion that one shows respect by refraining from criticizing another person's expressed religious ideas, no matter how out of touch with reality, has a noble history. It is a legacy from the days when religion was understood as a private concern, like the details of one's marriage. During that era, many Americans learned to give all religious ideas "a pass." In keeping with this tradition, we commonly subject to critical scrutiny ideas about almost everything except religion. If we hear someone say that women cannot do first-rate science, or that African Americans are just not as smart as Korean Americans, or that taxation is essentially a form of theft, or that the Americans won World War II with minimal help from the Soviets, or that global warming is a hoax, it is okay to challenge the speaker with evidence and reasoning. Not so with any idea presented as an aspect of someone's religious faith.

One might suppose that we live in a world of either/or: *either* religious ideas are relevant to public policy and thus subject to critical discussion, *or* they are not relevant and thus not a topic for debate. But instead, we live in a world of both/and: religious ideas are *both* relevant to public policy *and* excluded from critical evaluation.[8]

It is easy to disparage the hope for honest conversation about religious ideas. To doubt the power of argumentation about virtually any contested topic is often invoked as a mark of sophistication. But forthright debate has been basic to American democracy since Jefferson invoked "a decent respect for the opinions of mankind." Democracies give up on argumentation at their peril.

To be sure, truths about the world are more easily accepted when advanced by members of one's own tribe. Intellect works best when accompanied by fellow feeling. But tribal boundaries sometimes change, and tribal epistemologies are not beyond challenge. In the history of the United States, demographic diversification and epistemic demystification have together enabled many people to change their minds.[9] Religion is not impervious to argumentation, especially as informed by education.

Education is no guarantee against authoritarianism, as the history of right-wing regimes in modern Europe proves. But the more knowledge people gain about history, society, and nature—as distinguished from technical and vocational training, which has less decisive consequences for citizenship—the greater their capacity to evaluate the claims and counterclaims that always confront voters in a democracy. "Democracy must be born anew every generation," said John Dewey, "and education is its midwife."[10] When schooling is hard to come by, generous personal instincts and mutually supportive local communities can promote sound civic policies. But today, when highly capitalized programs of disinformation threaten to twist the common sense of the most honest and virtuous of souls, the need for education is especially great. "People here in the heartland," remarked the white Appalachian bard Joe Bageant on behalf of his ancestral tribe, "will keep electing dangerous dimwits in cowboy boots, until it is possible to get an education without going into crushing debt." Bageant added that "Malcolm X had it straight when he said that the first step in revolution is massive education of the people."[11]

Historical sociologists Claude Fischer and Michael Hout find that education more than any other measurable factor has separated Americans from one another in virtually all domains of human striving during the past one hundred years.[12] This applies with special significance to religion. Education makes people less inclined to ascribe to supernatural authority whatever value they find in the teachings and social function of Protestant and Catholic churches and less prone to invoke supernatural authority as a warrant for policing the worldly conduct of their fellow citizens. Worldliness is available to all, of course, no matter how much or how little time a person may have spent in school or how much experience a person may have had outside their tribe. Not everyone with a limited education is attracted to supernatural authority. In order to be an atheist or an agnostic, or to become indifferent to religion, you don't have to go to college or to be a world traveler.

What matters about religion for the health of democracy is not belief in God but what believers say God authorizes them to do. Millions of Americans profess faith in God but organize their public and private lives around worldly authorities informed by modern learning and refrain from accusing their political opponents of failing to obey authority located beyond human argumentation.[13] In a society where churches have long been vital centers of community, sustainers of cultural tradition, and settings in which to contemplate some of life's terrors and enigmas, it is not surprising that many individuals remain connected to churches even when any link to the supernatural is remote, or even nonexistent. The belief/nonbelief, religion/secular distinction can conceal the messiness of many people's spiritual strivings.

Before white evangelicals succeeded in getting so much of the country to treat them as the chief owners of Christianity, institutionally empowered ecumenical Protestants showed that divinity could be understood in keeping with what human beings have come to know about the world through schooling and through the expanded sense of humanity that comes from direct education in its varieties. These "other Protestants" sought to develop versions of Christianity that could work within a political system willingly shared with Jews, with other kinds of non-Christians, and with nonbelievers.

These campaigners for a more cosmopolitan Protestantism are the central actors in Christianity's relation to public affairs in the United States during the past one hundred years. They defined the terms of the ecumenical-evangelical divide. Did these people do as much as they might have to diminish racism, sexism, imperialism, Orientalism, homophobia, and anti-intellectualism? Certainly not. But this book has not put a fine point on this obvious truth because so little reflection is required to discover that a given cast of historical actors fails to measure up to today's sense of how people should behave. The ease with which we can answer this morally *structural* question—is someone within our ethical community, or not?—accounts for the question's copious and confident responses.

Morally *developmental* questions are more challenging. What conditions have facilitated the expansion of our ethical community? What has enabled equality, inclusion, and democracy to make what gains they have made? This book has attended to differences in education, theology, class position, and cross-cultural contact as major factors explaining why ecumenical Protestant leaders did more than most of their white Christian contemporaries to advance goals more easily affirmed today than when most of this book's subjects were active. The mainline leaders managed to do what they did not because of purity of heart, although some did have great generosity of spirit. They lived in a force field where descent and doctrine, wealth and war, trade and travel, science and sentiment, and a host of other elements in motion made them into the relatively well educated, relatively global individuals they became. The ecumenical Protestants emerge from this book less as heroic agents than as historic witnesses to the power of the forces that shaped and directed them.

American Protestants have always been subject to conflicting appeals, voiced by two of Christianity's greatest figures, the Apostle Paul and Immanuel Kant. Hold fast to the revealed truth, trusting that it can handle all earthly storms? Or conclude that those storms can overtake you unless you acquire worldly knowledge of them? Maintain the clearly bounded, rule-following Christian community Paul founded, risking that it will prove less viable than other, more capacious communities? Or try to build the universal moral and epistemic solidarity envisioned by Kant, risking loss of identity in a seemingly boundless expanse?

Most groups of American Protestants split the difference between Paul and Kant, somehow balancing their variously measured suspicions of a provincialism too confining and a cosmopolitanism too uncertain of its own destination. But eventually the two appeals became more sharply differentiated and drew constituencies increasingly separate from one another. The more control white evangelicals achieved over the Christian franchise and the more they allowed it to weaken democracy and to discredit science, the more comfortable other Americans came to feel in one another's spiritually and ethnoracially diverse company. The lines distinguishing liberal adherents of Protestantism, Catholicism, and Judaism from post-Protestants, post-Catholics, post-Judaic Jews, and other secularists became fuzzier. The secular emerged as less a threat than the sectarian to an inclusive national community committed to democracy. Paul's legacy was far from dead in the national arena, but Kant's was stronger there than ever, making white evangelical Protestantism's demographically disproportionate power in public affairs all the more paradoxical, and all the more demanding of critical engagement.

NOTES

Chapter 1. Introduction: The Other Protestants

1. John Barton, *A History of the Bible: The Story of the World's Most Influential Book* (New York, 2019), and Bart D. Ehrman, *A Brief Introduction to the New Testament*, 4th ed. (New York, 2017) are two excellent guides to the current state of biblical scholarship. See also Konrad Schmid and Jens Schroter, *The Making of the Bible: From the First Fragments to Sacred Scripture* (Cambridge, MA, 2021).

2. See especially four excellent studies: Katherine Stewart, *The Power Worshippers: Inside the Dangerous Rise of Religious Nationalism* (New York, 2019); Kristin Kobes Du Mez, *Jesus and John Wayne: How White Evangelicals Corrupted a Faith and Fractured a Nation* (New York, 2020); John Fea, *Believe Me: The Evangelical Road to Donald Trump* (Grand Rapids, MI, 2018); and Sarah Posner, *Unholy: Why White Evangelicals Worship at the Altar of Donald Trump* (New York, 2020).

3. William R. Hutchison, ed., *Between the Times: The Travail of the Protestant Establishment in America, 1900–1960* (New York, 1989) remains after more than three decades a valuable collection of scholarly studies of this wing of American Protestantism.

4. I have discussed these terminological issues in *After Cloven Tongues of Fire: Protestant Liberalism in Modern American History* (Princeton, 2013), xiii–xiv, and in *Protestants Abroad: How Missionaries Tried to Change World but Changed America* (Princeton, 2017), 10–11.

5. This perspective has been developed by N. J. Demerath III, "Cultural Victory and Organizational Defeat in the Paradoxical Decline of Liberal Protestantism," *Journal for the Scientific Study of Religion* 34 (1995), 458–469. See also Christian Smith and Patricia Snell, *Souls in Transition: The Religious and Spiritual Lives of Emerging Adults* (New York, 2009), esp. 187–188.

6. This theory was advanced with the greatest notice by Dean M. Kelley, *Why Conservative Churches Are Growing: A Study in the Sociology of Religion* (New York, 1972).

7. Pew Research Center, "More White Americans Adopted Than Shed Evangelical Label during Trump Presidency, Especially His Supporters," September 15, 2021,

https://www.pewresearch.org/fact-tank/2021/09/15/more-white-americans
-adopted-than-shed-evangelical-label-during-trump-presidency-especially-his
-supporters/. The findings of the Pew study are convincingly analyzed by political
scientist Ryan Burge, "Why 'Evangelical' Is Becoming Another Word for 'Republican,'" *New York Times*, October 31, 2021. 2

8. Craig Melvin, "'Enlightenment Is on the Ballot': Jon Meacham on Upcoming
Elections," *MSNBC*, June 22, 2020, https://www.msnbc.com/craig-melvin/watch/
-enlightenment-is-on-the-ballot-jon-meacham-on-upcoming-elections-85701701687.

9. "Why Obama Fears for Our Democracy," *Atlantic*, November 15, 2020. Of the
many other writers who have addressed this crisis, one of the most trenchant is So-
phia Rosenfeld, *Democracy and Truth: A Short History* (Philadelphia, 2019).

10. Jonathan Rauch, *The Constitution of Knowledge: A Defense of Truth* (Washington, DC, 2021) is one of many works exposing epistemic closure on the secular left
as well as the religious right. See also John McWhorter, *Woke Racism: How a New
Religion Has Betrayed Black Americans* (New York, 2021).

11. Mark Noll, quoted by Peter Wehner, "The Evangelical Church Is Breaking
Apart: Christians Must Reclaim Jesus from His Church," *Atlantic*, October 24, 2021,
https://www.theatlantic.com/ideas/archive/2021/10/evangelical-trump-christians
-politics/620469/. This essay by Wehner, a leading anti-Trump evangelical writer,
exemplifies the common impulse to downplay, if not actually deny, the connection
between evangelicalism's history and its current appeal to pro-Trump Republicans.

12. "NIH Director: 'Our Culture Wars Are Killing People,'" PBS, November 3, 2021,
https://www.pbs.org/video/nih-director-our-culture-wars-are-killing-people-dpyfnx/.

13. For a judicious commentary on how the history of evangelical thought renders
QAnon's claims believable, see Christopher Douglas, "Revenge Is a Genre Best Served
Old: Apocalypse in Christian Right Literature and Politics," *Religion* 13 (2021).

14. Jill Lepore, *These Truths: A History of the United States* (New York, 2018), xiv.

15. W. K. Clifford, *Lectures and Essays* (London, 1879), 346.

Chapter 2. A Country Protestant on Steroids

1. David Sehat, *The Myth of American Religious Freedom* (New York, 2011).

2. Writing in 1835, Tocqueville observed that "Americans so completely confuse
Christianity and freedom in their minds that it is almost impossible to have them
conceive of the one without the other." Alexis de Tocqueville, *Democracy in America*,
ed. Harvey Mansfield (Chicago, 2002), 280–281.

3. H. K. Carroll, ed., *The Religious Forces of the United States* (New York, 1896),
392.

4. Jon Butler, *Awash in a Sea of Faith: Christianizing the American People* (Cambridge, MA, 1990).

5. The impact on Weber of his trip of 1904 is detailed in Lawrence A. Scaff, *Max Weber in America* (Princeton, 2011).

6. Grover Cleveland as quoted in Martin E. Marty, *Modern American Religion*, vol. 1: *The Irony of It All, 1893–1919* (Chicago, 1986), 42.

7. Henry F. May, *The Enlightenment in America* (New York, 1976).

8. Andrew Dickson White, *A History of the Warfare of Science with Theology in Christendom* (New York, 1896).

9. US Department of Education, *120 Years of American Education: A Statistical Portrait* (Washington, 1993), 65.

10. David Bebbington, "Evangelism and Secularization in Britain and America from the Eighteenth Century to the Present," in David Hempton and Hugh McLeod, eds., *Secularization and Religious Innovation in the North Atlantic World* (New York, 2017), 77.

11. Martin E. Marty, *Righteous Empire: The Protestant Experience in America* (New York, 1970), 177–179.

12. Richard Hofstadter, *Anti-intellectualism in American Life* (New York, 1964), 118.

13. Amanda Porterfield, *Conceived in Doubt: Religion and Politics in the New American Nation* (Chicago, 2012), 12.

14. John Fea, *Believe Me: The Evangelical Road to Donald Trump* (Grand Rapids, MI, 2018), 101, emphasis original.

Chapter 3. Jewish Immigrants versus Anglo-Protestant Hegemony

1. I have addressed this event more extensively in my *Science, Jews, and Secular Culture: Studies in Mid-Twentieth-Century American Intellectual History* (Princeton, 1996). See also my defense of the practice of openly recognizing the cultural impact of this non-Christian population, "Rich, Powerful, and Smart: Jewish Overrepresentation Should Be Explained Rather Than Avoided or Mystified," *Jewish Quarterly Review* 94 (2004), 594–602.

2. Randolph Bourne, "The Jew and Transnational America," *Menorah Journal* 2 (1916), 277–284, esp. 284; Randolph Bourne, "Trans-National America," *Atlantic* 118 (1916), 86–97.

3. Hutchins Hapgood, *The Spirit of the Ghetto* (New York, 1909); Thorstein Veblen, "The Intellectual Preeminence of Jews in Modern Europe," *Political Science Quarterly* 34 (1919), 33–42.

4. Madison Grant, *The Passing of the Great Race* (New York, 1916).

5. C. Luther Fry, ed., *1933 Year Book of the Churches* (New York, 1933), 311–316, as cited by William R. Hutchison, ed., *Between the Times: The Travail of the Protestant Establishment in America, 1900–1960* (New York, 1989), 17.

6. Dan A. Oren, *Joining the Club: A History of Jews and Yale* (New Haven, CT, 1985), 326.

7. The results of the Carnegie study, which was designed by sociologist Martin Trow, are reported in Stephen Steinberg, *The Academic Melting Pot: Catholics and Jews in American Higher Education* (New York, 1974).

8. Bruce Kuklick, *From Churchmen to Philosophers* (New Haven, CT, 1985), is the standard treatment of this development.

9. William James, *The Varieties of Religious Experience* (New York, 1902); Josiah Royce, *The Problem of Christianity* (New York, 1913).

10. "Humanist Manifesto," *New Humanist*, May 1933. The Protestant matrix for the manifesto is extensively explored by Stephen P. Weldon, *The Scientific Spirit of American Humanism* (Baltimore, 2020), 53–61.

11. Morris R. Cohen's most important works were *Reason and Nature: An Essay on the Meaning of Scientific Method* (New York, 1931) and *Law and the Social Order: Essays in Legal Philosophy* (New York, 1933). I have addressed his career in my *Morris R. Cohen and the Scientific Ideal* (Cambridge, MA, 1975).

12. "How Today's Thinkers Serve Society," *National Observer*, July 20, 1964, 18. This article was called to my attention by Laurie Shrage.

13. Walter Kaufmann, *A Critique of Religion and Philosophy* (New York, 1958), 302.

14. Christian Smith, "Introduction," in Christian Smith, ed., *The Secular Revolution: Power, Interests, and Conflict in the Secularization of American Public Life* (Berkeley, CA, 2003), 47.

15. Robert F. Goheen, "The Seminary and the University," *Princeton Seminary Bulletin*, July 1960, quoted in Clyde A. Holbrook, ed., *Religion: A Humanistic Field* (Princeton, 1963), 24. Born to missionary parents in India, Goheen as president of Princeton worked to diminish racial, religious, and gender prejudice at that institution. Under his leadership, women were admitted for the first time as undergraduates.

16. Andrew Abbott, *The System of Professions: An Essay on the Division of Expert Labor* (Chicago, 1988), 308–309, 313.

17. Edwin S. Gaustad, "The Pulpit and the Pews," in William R. Hutchison, ed., *Between the Times: The Travail of the Protestant Establishment in America, 1900–1960* (New York, 1989), 31.

18. Leslie A. Fiedler, "Master of Dreams: The Jew in a Gentile World," *Partisan Review*, Summer 1967, as reprinted in Fiedler, *To the Gentiles* (New York, 1971), 183.

19. Neal Gabler, *An Empire of Their Own: How the Jews Invented Hollywood* (New York, 1988), 6.

20. The percentage of Jews in many professions and institutions is documented in Seymour Martin Lipset and Earl Raab, *Jews and the American Scene* (Cambridge, MA, 1995). Lipset and Raab note that of the American scientists who won a Nobel Prize before 1965, 27 percent were Jewish.

21. Doug McAdam, *Freedom Summer* (New York, 1990).

22. Joyce Antler, *Jewish Radical Feminism: Voices from the Women's Liberation Movement* (New York, 2018), 11. For a discerning discussion of the relative lack of Protestant feminists and attention to some important cases, see Anne Braude, "A Religious Feminist—Who Can Find Her? Historiographical Challenges from the National Organization of Women," *Journal of Religion* 84 (2004), 555–572.

23. Will Herberg, *Protestant-Catholic-Jew: An Essay in Religious Sociology* (New York, 1955).

24. K. Healan Gaston, *Imagining Judeo-Christian America: Religion, Secularism, and the Redefinition of Democracy* (Chicago, 2019).

25. Steinberg, *Academic Melting Pot*, 141.

26. A lucid account of the church-and-state suits brought by Pfeffer, and of the rulings of the US Supreme Court that followed, is found in David Sehat, *This Earthly Frame: The Making of American Secularism* (New Haven, CT, 2022).

27. Samuel Walker, *In Defense of American Liberties: A History of the ACLU* (New York, 1990), 220.

28. "Billy Graham Responds to Lingering Anger over 1972 Remarks on Jews," *New York Times*, March 17, 2002, reports on the National Archives' release of tapes of this conversation of fifty years before and the ensuing controversy. Graham had vigorously denied having ever spoken about Jews, with Nixon or anyone else, except "in the most positive" terms.

29. Roy J. Harris, Jr., "The Best-Selling Record of All," *Wall Street Journal*, December 11, 2009.

30. Philip Roth, *Operation Shylock: A Confession* (New York, 1993), 157.

31. T. S. Eliot, *After Strange Gods* (London, 1934).

Chapter 4. The Missionary Boomerang

1. C. Howard Hopkins, *John R. Mott, 1865–1955* (Geneva, 1985), 665.

2. Mark Twain, *Innocents Abroad* (New York, 1869), 493.

3. I have addressed this "boomerang effect" of Protestant foreign missions on American public life in my *Protestants Abroad: How Missionaries Tried to Change the World but Changed America* (Princeton, 2017).

4. Melani McAlister, *The Kingdom of God Has No Borders: A Global History of American Evangelicalism* (New York, 2018), 46.

5. See, for example, Soojin Chung, *Adopting for God: The Mission to Change America through Transracial Adoption* (New York, 2021).

6. For an account of Kagawa's role in the antiracist campaign of ecumenicals, see David P. King, "The West Looks East: The Influence of Tohohiko Kagawa on American Mainline Protestants," *Church History* 80 (2011), 302–320.

7. Carl F. Bowman, *Brethren Society: The Cultural Transformation of a "Peculiar People"* (Baltimore, 1995), 388.

8. Pearl Buck, *The Good Earth* (New York, 1931). Will Rogers is quoted by Peter Conn, *Pearl S. Buck: A Cultural Biography* (Cambridge, MA, 1996), 153. Paul Hutchinson, "Breeder of Life," *Christian Century*, May 20, 1931, 683. For the comparison to Marco Polo, see James Claude Thomson Jr., "Pearl S. Buck and the American Quest for China," in Elisabeth J. Lipscomb et al., eds., *The Several Worlds of Pearl S. Buck: Essays Presented at a Centennial Symposium* (Westport, CT, 1994), 14.

9. Hilary Spurling, *Pearl Buck in China: Journey to the Good Earth* (New York, 2010), 228–229.

10. John Hersey, *Hiroshima* (New York, 1946).

11. Jeremy Treglown, *Mr. Straight Arrow: The Career of John Hersey, Author of Hiroshima* (New York, 2019), 136.

12. Henry Luce, "The American Century," *Life*, February 17, 1941; Henry Wallace, *The Century of the Common Man* (New York, 1943).

13. In a typical flourish, Wallace concluded the speech of May 8, 1942, which became the basis for his book of 1943, in an entirely biblical voice. "No compromise with Satan is possible. . . . The People's revolution is on the march, and the devil and all his angels cannot prevail against it. They cannot prevail, for on the side of the people is the Lord." Henry Wallace, "The Century of the Common Man," in *Prefaces to Peace* (New York, 1943), 375.

14. Jane Hong, *Opening the Gates to Asia: A Transpacific History of How America Repealed Asian Exclusion* (Chapel Hill, NC, 2019).

15. Sherwood Moran, *Suggestions for Japanese Interpreters Based on Work in the Field* (First Marine Division, July 17, 1943).

16. Hugh Milford, *America's Great Game: The CIA's Secret Arabists and the Shaping of the Modern Middle East* (New York, 2013), 276, 288.

17. Margaret Landon, *Anna and the King of Siam* (New York, 1944).

18. Daniel J. Fleming, *Whither Missions* (New York, 1925).

19. E. Stanley Jones, *The Christ of the Indian Road* (London, 1925); E. Stanley Jones, *Mahatma Gandhi: An Interpretation* (New York, 1948), 77.

20. Edmund D. Soper, *The Religions of Mankind* (New York, 1921). Other works in this tradition included Robert E. Hume, *World Living Religions* (New York, 1924), and Huston Smith, *The World's Religions: Our Great Wisdom Tradition* (New York, 1958).

21. William Ernest Hocking, *Re-Thinking Missions: A Laymen's Inquiry after One Hundred Years* (New York, 1932).

22. William Ernest Hocking, *The Meaning of God in Human Experience* (New Haven, CT, 1912).

23. William Ernest Hocking, *The Spirit of World Politics* (New York, 1932), 8, as quoted by John Stuart, "Empire, Mission, Ecumenism, and Human Rights," *Church History* 83 (2014), 119.

24. Hocking, *Re-Thinking Missions*, 65, 67, 70, 77, 246, 254.

25. Frederick Bohn Fisher, "Re-Thinking Missions," *Christian Century*, December 12, 1932.

26. Hocking, *Re-Thinking Missions*, 29, 40, 44.

27. H. Richard Niebuhr, *The Social Sources of Denominationalism* (New York, 1929), 280.

28. Sherwood Eddy, "Church Union in India," *Christian Century*, March 28, 1920, 13.

29. Henry P. Van Dusen, *World Christianity: Yesterday, Today, Tomorrow* (New York, 1947), 288.

Chapter 5. The Apotheosis of Liberal Protestantism

1. John C. Bennett, *Christians and the State* (New York, 1958), 5, 22, 187.

2. "Christian Amendment," in *Hearings Before a Subcommittee of the Committee on the Judiciary of the United States Senate, on S. J. Res 87, May 13 and 17, 1954*, 78–79.

3. Michael G. Thompson, *For God and Globe: Christian Internationalism in the United States between the Great War and the Cold War* (Ithaca, NY, 2015); Or Rosenboim, *The Emergence of Globalism: Visions of World Order in Britain and the United States, 1939–1950* (Princeton, 2017); Gene Zubovich, *Before the Religious Right: Liberal Protestants, Human Rights, and the Polarization of the United States* (Philadelphia, 2022).

4. While the Social Gospel was largely a middle-class movement, like the political Progressive movement with which it was closely allied, recent scholarship has established that much of the impetus for the Social Gospel came from working-class Americans, including craftsmen and trade unionists. See especially Heath Carter, *Union Made: Working People and the Rise of Social Christianity in Chicago* (New York, 2015), and the symposium, "State of the Field of Social Gospel Studies," *Church History* 84 (2015), 195–219.

5. James 2:18.

6. George M. Marsden, *Fundamentalism and American Culture: The Shaping of Twentieth-Century Evangelicalism, 1870–1925* (New York, 1980), 4.

7. Timothy E. W. Gloege, *Guaranteed Pure: The Moody Bible Institute, Business, and the Making of Modern Evangelicalism* (Chapel Hill, NC, 2015), is a helpful guide to the ways in which the fundamentalist movement was innovative, rather than a straightforward extension of nineteenth-century theological conservatism.

8. Sandra C. Taylor, *Advocate of Understanding: Sidney Gulick and the Search for Peace with Japan* (Kent, OH, 1984).

9. See Kelley J. Baker, *Gospel According to the Klan* (Lawrence, KS, 2011). For a helpful reminder that early fundamentalism had a large following in urban as well as rural and small-town America, see Wallace Best, "Battle for the Soul of a City: John Roach Straton, Harry Emerson Fosdick, and the Fundamentalist-Modernist Controversy in New York, 1922–1935," *Church History* 90 (2021), 367–397.

10. Reinhold Niebuhr, *Moral Man and Immoral Society* (New York, 1932).

11. Edmund D. Soper, quoted in *Time*, November 8, 1926.

12. Matthew Avery Sutton, *American Apocalypse: A History of Modern Evangelicalism* (Cambridge, MA, 2014), has shown that fundamentalist preachers and laymen put money into far-right organizations and schools and often attacked the New Deal as "the anti-Christ," reflecting the strong Manichean tendency of fundamentalists to treat their enemies as evil rather than rivals within a single community.

13. Darren Dochuk, *Anointed with Oil: How Christianity and Crude Made Modern America* (New York, 2019), is a brilliant study of the connection between evangelical religion and antiregulation politics long before, as well as after, World War II.

14. Luke 10:25–37.

15. Dulles's historic role as an ecumenical Protestant leader remains largely unrecognized, overshadowed by his later prominence as secretary of state. A helpful study is Bevan Sewell, "Pragmatism, Religion, and John Foster Dulles' Embrace of Christian Internationalism in the 1930s," *Diplomatic History* 41 (2017), 799–823.

16. "American Malvern," *Time*, March 16, 1942.

17. Samuel Moyn, *Christian Human Rights* (Philadelphia, 2015), 148.

18. This included freedom from police brutality and mob violence, the right to employment, the right to join a labor union, the right to receive equal services, and the right to participate fully in government institutions, including the military. Gene Zubovich, "Human Rights Abroad, against Jim Crow at Home: The Political Mobilization of the American Ecumenical Protestants in the World War II Era," *Journal of American History* 105 (2018), 267. See also Zubovich, *Before the Religious Right*.

19. Frederick Nolde, ed., *Toward World-Wide Christianity* (New York, 1946), 142.

20. Federal Council of Churches, *The Church and Race Relations: An Official Statement Approved by the Federal Council of the Churches of Christ in America at a Special Meeting, Columbus, Ohio, March 5–7, 1946* (New York, 1946).

21. The role of these African Americans in the ecumenical leadership is discerningly analyzed by David W. Willis, "An Enduring Distance: Black Americans and the Establishment," in William R. Hutchison, ed., *Between the Times: The Travail of the Protestant Establishment in America, 1900–1960* (New York, 1989), 168–192, and by Dennis C. Dickerson, "African American Religious Intellectuals and the Theological Foundations of the Civil Rights Movement, 1930–55," *Church History* 74 (2005), 217–235.

22. Joseph Kip Kosek, *Acts of Conscience: Christians, Nonviolence, and Modern American Democracy* (New York, 2009), 204–208.

23. Virginia L. Brereton, "United and Slighted: Women as Subordinated Insiders," in Hutchison, *Between the Times*, 155.

24. Martin E. Marty, *Modern American Religion*, vol. 3: *Under God, Indivisible, 1941–1960* (Chicago, 1996), 247. The most comprehensive and discerning study of organized churchwomen is Margaret Bendroth, *Good and Mad: Mainline Protestant Churchwomen, 1920–1980* (New York, 2022).

25. Buell G. Gallagher, *Color and Conscience: The Irrepressible Conflict* (New York, 1946); Edmund D. Soper, *Racism: A World Issue* (New York, 1947).

26. Marty, *Modern American Religion*, 266.

27. Sara M. Evans, "Introduction," in Evans, ed., *Journeys That Opened Up the World: Women, Student Christian Movements, and Social Justice, 1955–1975* (New Brunswick, NJ, 2003), 9.

28. M. Richard Shaull, *Encounter with Revolution* (New York, 1955).

29. Bennett, *Christians and the State*, 22.

30. Eisenhower's statement of 1952 is often quoted out of context as an emblem for the apparent blandness of the era. But historian Patrick Henry has established that Eisenhower made this remark in the context of an antisectarian affirmation of the equality of all faiths; see Henry, "'And I Don't Care What It Is': The Tradition-History of a Civil Religion Proof-Text," *Journal of the American Academy of Religion* 49 (1981), 35–49.

31. Reinhold Niebuhr, *The Irony of American History* (New York, 1952), 174.

32. E.g., Elizabeth Samet, *Looking for the Good War: American Amnesia and the Violent Pursuit of Happiness* (New York, 2021), 221–224.

33. I have tried to clarify Niebuhr's historical significance in my *After Cloven Tongues of Fire: Protestant Liberalism in Modern American History* (Princeton, 2013), 211–225.

34. Paul Tillich, *Theology of Culture* (New York, 1959), 176.

35. Dochuk, *Anointed with Oil*, and Kevin Kruse, *One Nation under God: How Corporate America Invented Christian America* (New York, 2015).

36. E. Earl Ellis, "Segregation and the Kingdom of God," *Christianity Today*, March 18, 1957. The willingness of Carl Henry and other evangelical leaders involved in the launching of *Christianity Today* to make their peace with the Jim Crow regime of the South is copiously documented by Daniel Silliman, "An Evangelical Is Anyone Who Likes Billy Graham: Defining Evangelicalism with Carl Henry and Networks of Trust," *Church History* 90 (2021), esp. 640–641.

37. Charles C. F. Henry, "Why Is the NCC Prestige Sagging?," *Christianity Today*, February 2, 1959, 5. See also William Inboden, *Religion and American Foreign Policy, 1945–1960: The Soul of Containment* (New York, 2008), esp. 95–99.

38. Grant Wacker, *America's Pastor: Billy Graham and the Shaping of a Nation* (Cambridge, MA, 2014), 39. Wacker's study of Graham is the best ever written, but

174 NOTES TO CHAPTER 6

by calling Graham "America's Pastor" Wacker too nearly erases the America that Wacker himself acknowledges had no use for Graham. Moreover, Wacker refuses to hold Graham accountable for his role in licensing the anti-intellectualism and cultural complacency that profoundly affected the shape of American evangelicalism and, in turn, the "nation" of Wacker's subtitle. For sharply contrasting critical assessments of this important book, see the reviews by Robert P. George, *New York Times,* December 21, 2014, and by myself, *Christian Century,* October 15, 2014. See also my "Billy Graham's Missed Opportunities," *New York Times,* February 18, 2018.

39. Reinhold Niebuhr, "Differing Views on Billy Graham: A Theologian Says Evangelist Is Simplifying Views on Life," *Life,* July 1, 1957, 92.

40. Shaun A. Casey, *The Making of a Catholic President: Kennedy vs. Nixon 1960* (New York, 2009), 184.

41. "Protestantism's Third Phase," *Christian Century,* January 18, 1961, 72.

42. Daniel Hummel shows how embedded evangelical support for Israel was in the notion of a Judeo-Christian tradition, which in the evangelical formulation embraced Zionism as a religious movement; see Hummel, *Covenant Brothers: Evangelicals, Jews, and U.S.-Israeli Relations* (Philadelphia, 2019).

Chapter 6. The 1960s and the Decline of the Mainline

1. William Stringfellow, *My People Is the Enemy: An Autobiographical Polemic* (New York, 1964); Gibson Winter, *The Suburban Captivity of the Churches* (New York, 1961).

2. Ralph Dodge, *The Unpopular Missionary* (New York, 1964).

3. James Scherer, *Missionary, Go Home! A Reappraisal of the Christian World Mission* (New York, 1964).

4. Wilfred Cantwell Smith, "Christianity's Third Great Challenge," *Christian Century,* April 27, 1960, 505.

5. Gabriel Vahanian, *The Death of God: The Culture of Our Post-Christian Era* (New York, 1961); Paul M. Van Buren, *The Secular Meaning of the Gospel* (New York, 1963); "The God Is Dead Movement," *Time,* October 22, 1965.

6. John A. T. Robinson, *Honest to God* (London, 1963), 66.

7. John C. Bennett, "A Most Welcome Event," *Christianity and Crisis,* November 11, 1963, 202.

8. Harvey Cox, *The Secular City* (New York, 1965), 266, 268. A sampling of the animated discussion of Cox's book was edited the following year by Daniel Callahan, *The Secular City Debate* (New York, 1966).

9. Cox, *Secular City,* 99.

10. The definitive study of this episode in progressive activism by ecumenical Protestant leaders is Jill K. Gill, *Embattled Ecumenism: The National Council of Churches, the Vietnam War, and the Trials of the Protestant Left* (DeKalb, IL, 2011).

11. Graham, quoted in Anthea Butler, *White Evangelical Racism: The Politics of Morality in America* (Chapel Hill, NC, 2021), 34.

12. The ecumenical-evangelical divide on civil rights is extensively documented in Jesse Curtis, *The Myth of Colorblind Christians: Evangelicals and White Supremacy in the Civil Rights Era* (New York, 2021). For the often hidden connection between white supremacy and the theological doctrine of biblical inerrancy, see Stephen Young, "Biblical Inerrancy's Long History as an Evangelical Activist for White Patriarchy," *Religion Dispatches*, February 9, 2022.

13. This construction was popularized by Taylor Branch's three-volume work, *America in the King Years* (New York, 1988–2006).

14. J. Edgar Hoover, "The Communist Menace: Red Goals and Christian Ideals," *Christianity Today*, October 10, 1960, 3–5. Hoover's later articles appeared in the issues following.

15. A book of 1969 brought into focus this developing but often ignored reality: Jeffrey K. Hadden, *The Gathering Storm in the Churches: A Sociologist Looks at the Widening Gap Between Clergy and Laymen* (New York, 1969).

16. Dean R. Hoge, Benton Johnson, and Donald A. Luidens, *Vanishing Boundaries: The Religion of Mainline Protestant Baby Boomers* (Louisville, 1994), 2.

17. General Social Survey, as cited by Ryan P. Burge, *The Nones: Where They Came From, Who They Are, and Where They Are Going* (Minneapolis, 2021), 19. For the purpose of these surveys, demographers count seven major denominations as "mainline": United Methodists, Evangelical (misleadingly named) Lutherans, Presbyterians, Episcopalians, Northern Baptists, Disciples of Christ, and United Church of Christ. A number of smaller confessions continued to have much in common with "the seven sisters," including the Quakers, the Church of the Brethren, the Dutch Reformed, and—although not always considered Christian—the Unitarian-Universalists.

18. General Social Survey, "Social Change Report 26," https://gss.norc.org /Documents/reports/social-change-reports/SC26.pdf.

19. Walter Lippmann, "The University," *New Republic*, May 28, 1966, 17–20.

20. Robert Wuthnow, *The Restructuring of American Religion: Society and Faith since World War II* (Princeton, 1988), 162.

21. Nicholas Wolterstorff, "Epilogue," in Andrea Sterk, ed., *Religion, Scholarship, and Higher Education: Perspectives, Models, and Future Prospects* (Notre Dame, IN, 2002), 249, emphasis original. My own critique of the Lilly Seminar on Religion and Higher Education, in which I participated, is "Enough Already: American Universities Do Not Need More Christianity," also included in Sterk, *Religion, Scholarship, and Higher Education*, 40–49.

22. Dorothy Bass, "Revolutions, Quiet and Otherwise: Protestants and Higher Education during the 1960s," in Parker J. Palmer, Barbara G. Wheeler, and James W.

Fowler, eds., *Caring for the Commonwealth: Education for Religious and Public Life* (Atlanta, 1990), 209.

23. Michael Hout, Andrew Greeley, and Melissa J. Wilde, "The Demographic Imperative of Religious Change in the United States," *American Journal of Sociology* 107 (2001), 468–500.

24. The latest studies show the continued aging of ecumenical churches. In 2019, the National Congregations Study found that 57 percent of members of ecumenical congregations were over sixty, while only 39 percent of evangelical church members were. Mark Chaves et al., *Congregations in 21st Century America* (Durham, NC, 2021), 42.

25. Kristy L. Slominski, *Teaching Moral Sex: A History of Religion and Sex Education in the United States* (New York, 2021), 3.

26. R. Marie Griffith, *Moral Combat: How Sex Divided American Christians and Fractured American Politics* (New York, 2017).

27. Everyone who writes about the Southern Strategy is indebted to Rick Perlstein, "Lee Atwater's Infamous Interview on the Southern Strategy," *Nation*, November 13, 2012. The best study is Angie Maxwell and Todd Shields, *The Long Southern Strategy: How Chasing White Voters in the South Changed American Politics* (New York, 2021), which calls attention to the initial steps taken in the Republican Party circles of Barry Goldwater, prior even to Nixon and his advisors.

28. "The Religious States of America," *Washington Post*, February 26, 2015.

Chapter 7. Ecumenical Democrats, Evangelical Republicans, and Post-Protestants

1. Josh Hawley, speech of 2017, as quoted in Katherine Stewart, "The Roots of Josh Hawley's Rage," *New York Times*, January 11, 2021. The popularity of this outlook in evangelical churches was a frequent theme of journalists in the wake of the 2020 election; see, for example, Stephanie McCrummen, "An American Kingdom," *Washington Post*, July 12, 2021, https://www.washingtonpost.com/nation/2021/07/11/mercy-culture-church/.

2. Wilfred Cantwell Smith, "Christianity's Third Great Challenge," *Christian Century*, April 27, 1960, 505.

3. The scriptural warrant for this outlook is the vehemently sectarian imperative of 2 Corinthians 10:5, where the Apostle Paul demands that the disciples "cast down" all unfaithful impulses and "take captive every thought to make it obedient to Christ."

4. Randall Balmer, *Solemn Reverence: The Separation of Church and State in American Life* (Lebanon, NH, 2021), 77.

5. A concise, accessible overview of the history of this issue is Garry Wills, "The Bishops Are Wrong about Biden—and Abortion," *New York Times*, June 27, 2021,

https://www.nytimes.com/2021/06/27/opinion/biden-bishops-communion
-abortion.html?action=click&module=Well&pgtype=Homepage&section=Guest%20
Essays.

6. Linda Greenhouse and Reva B. Siegel, "Before (and After) *Roe v. Wade*: New Questions about Backlash," *Yale Law Journal* 120 (2011).

7. Anthea Butler, *White Evangelical Racism: The Politics of Morality in America* (Chapel Hill, NC, 2021), 83, 114.

8. George M. Marsden, "On Not Mistaking One Part for the Whole: The Future of American Evangelicalism in a Global Perspective," in Mark Noll et al., eds., *Evangelicals* (Grand Rapids, 2019), 282. A trenchant critique of Marsden and the other chief contributors to *Evangelicals* is Christopher D. Cantwell, "How the Study of Evangelicalism Has Blinded Us to the Problems in Evangelical Culture," *Religion Dispatches*, March 4, 2021, https://religiondispatches.org/how-the-study-of-evangelicalism-has-blinded-us-to-the-problems-in-evangelical-culture/.

9. For a discussion of premillennial dispensationalism's similarity to QAnon, see Andrew Gardner, "Why Are Christians so Susceptible to Conspiracy?," *Baptist News Global*, August 31, 2020. See also Adam Williams, "QAnon Didn't Just Spring Forth from the Void—It's the Latest from a Familiar Movement," *Religion Dispatches*, September 10, 2020, https://religiondispatches.org/qanon-didnt-just-spring-forth-from-the-void-its-the-latest-from-a-familiar-movement/.

10. Amanda Porterfield, "Bebbington's Approach to Evangelical Christianity as a Pioneering Effort in Lived Religion," in Noll et al., *Evangelicals*, 146. This volume also includes Bebbington's own "The Nature of Evangelical Religion," 31–55, and a round-table discussion of Bebbington's quadrilateral by six leading historians.

11. Kristin Kobes Du Mez, *Jesus and John Wayne: How White Evangelicals Corrupted a Faith and Fractured a Nation* (New York, 2020), 3.

12. Robert D. Putnam and David E. Campbell, *American Grace: How Religion Divides and Unites Us* (New York, 2010), 21–22, 26.

13. "White Evangelical Resistance Is Obstacle in the Push for Vaccinations," *New York Times*, April 5, 2021.

14. Molly Worthen, *Apostles of Reason: The Crisis of Authority in American Evangelicalism* (New York, 2014), 261, and Molly Worthen, "The Evangelical Roots of Our Post-Truth Society," *New York Times*, April 13, 2017.

15. George M. Marsden, *Fundamentalism and American Culture: The Shaping of Twentieth-Century Evangelicalism, 1870–1925* (New York, 1980), 56.

16. Worthen, *Apostles of Reason*, 2, 110.

17. Philip A. Djupe and Ryan P. Burge, "A Conspiracy and the Heart of It: Religion and Q," *Religion in Public*, November 6, 2020.

18. Alexander Theodoridis, quoted in Thomas B. Edsall, "Trump True Believers Have Their Reasons," *New York Times*, October 6, 2001.

19. Pat Robertson, *700 Club* broadcast of November 17, 2020, linked by Crissy Stroop, "Why Do So Many Evangelicals Continue to Deny That Biden Won the Election," *Conversationalist*, November 26, 2020, https://conversationalist.org/2020/11/26/many-evangelicals-continue-to-deny-that-biden-won-the-election/.

20. See the sympathetic study by David R. Swartz, *Moral Minority: The Evangelical Left in an Age of Conservatism* (Philadelphia, 2014).

21. "Evangelical Lobbyist Resigns," *New York Times*, December 12, 2008.

22. David P. Gushee, *After Evangelicalism: The Path to a New Christianity* (Louisville, KY, 2020). For Gushee's brief discussion of the ecumenical tradition, see 114 and 169.

23. Worthen, *Apostles of Reason*, 222.

24. Gary North, quoted in Katherine Stewart, *The Power Worshipers: Inside the Dangerous Rise of Religious Nationalism* (New York, 2019), 119.

25. The Kinzinger family letter was published in full in Reid J. Epstein, "Adam Kinzinger's Lonely Mission," *New York Times*, February 15, 2021.

26. John Fea, *Believe Me: The Evangelical Road to Donald Trump* (Grand Rapids, MI, 2018), 113.

27. Pew Research Center, "Faith on the Hill," February 4, 2021, https://www.pewforum.org/2021/01/04/faith-on-the-hill-2021/.

28. Pew Research Center, "In U.S., Decline of Christianity Continues at Record Pace" (October 17, 2019), https://www.pewforum.org/wp-content/uploads/sites/7/2019/10/Trends-in-Religious-Identity-and-Attendance-FOR-WEB-1.pdf. Some other surveys, phrasing the question differently, generated even higher percentages of nonaffiliates. The Cooperative Congressional Election Study of 2016 concluded that 31 percent of Americans had no religious affiliation. See Stephen Ansolabehere et al., "CCES Common Content, 2016," https://dataverse.harvard.edu/dataset.xhtml?persistentId=doi%3A10.7910/DVN/GDF6Z0.

29. Gregory A. Smith, "About Three-in-Ten U.S. Adults Are Now Religiously Unaffiliated" (Pew Research Center, December 14, 2021), https://www.pewforum.org/2021/12/14/about-three-in-ten-u-s-adults-are-now-religiously-unaffiliated/. See also Yonat Shimron, "More Americans Are Becoming Secular," *Washington Post*, December 16, 2021.

30. That the greater social acceptance of nonaffiliation accelerated the numbers of nones is a major point of Ryan P. Burge, *The Nones: Where They Came From, Who They Are, and Where They Are Going* (Minneapolis, 2021), esp. 42–46. For Burge's analysis of the increase of African American nonaffiliates, see 89–91. An extensive analysis of the internal composition of the nonaffiliating population is found in David E. Campbell, Geoffrey C. Layman, and John C. Green, *Secular Surge: A New Fault Line in American Politics* (New York, 2021).

31. For a useful summary of recent membership figures, see Ryan Burge, "Why It's Unlikely US Mainline Protestants Outnumber Evangelicals," *Religion Unplugged*,

July 12, 2021, https://religionunplugged.com/news/2021/7/12/why-its-unlikely-us-mainline-protestants-outnumber-evangelicals.

32. David P. Gushee, *After Evangelicalism: The Path to a New Christianity* (Louisville, 2020), 170.

33. Claude S. Fischer and Michael Hout, *Century of Difference: How America Changed in the Last One Hundred Years* (New York, 2006), 207.

34. Stephen Bullivant, *Mass Exodus: Catholic Disaffiliation in Britain and America since Vatican II* (New York, 2020).

35. Leslie Woodcock Tentler, *Catholics and Contraception: An American History* (Ithaca, NY, 2009).

36. Martin E. Marty, *Righteous Empire: The Protestant Experience in America* (New York, 1970), 264. Marty was also an early champion of the concept of "post-Protestant," e.g., in Martin E. Marty, *The New Shape of American Religion* (New York, 1959), 32.

37. Charlotte Bunch, "Charlotte Bunch," in Sara M. Evans, ed., *Journeys That Opened Up the World: Women, Student Christian Movements, and Social Justice, 1955–1975* (New Brunswick, NJ, 2003), 139.

38. Langdon Gilkey, "The Christian Congregation as a Religious Community," in James P. Wind and James W. Lewis, eds., *American Congregations: New Perspectives in the Study of Congregations* (Chicago, 1994), 105. Anthropologist Margaret Mead, often thought of as an entirely secular thinker, was a churchgoing Episcopalian who fit easily into Gilkey's description; see Elesha J. Coffman, *Margaret Mead: A Twentieth-Century Faith* (New York, 2021).

39. N. J. Demerath III, "Cultural Victory and Organizational Defeat in the Paradoxical Decline of Liberal Protestantism," *Journal for the Scientific Study of Religion* 34 (1995), 458–460.

40. P. Mackenzie Bok, "To the Mountaintop Again: The Early Rawls and Post-Protestant Ethics in Postwar America," *Modern Intellectual History* 14 (2017), 153–185.

Chapter 8. Christianity's American Fate: A Conservative Refuge?

1. Theo Hobson, "Not Liberal Enough," *Times Literary Supplement*, September 7, 2012, 23.

2. There were a few gestures toward unification. The Congregationalists and the German Reformed combined in 1957 to create the United Church of Christ. Several Lutheran synods merged to create the misleadingly titled Evangelical Lutheran Church in America, but in so doing they merely overcame ethnic divisions within a shared ancestry in Northwestern Europe. Other than small-group mergers here and there, that was it, except for the reuniting of demographically and theologically

homogeneous groups that had been divided over slavery. The Methodists reunited in 1939 and the Presbyterians in 1983.

3. Keith Watkins, *The American Church That Might Have Been: A History of the Consultation on Church Union* (Eugene, OR, 2014), 114. This book is one of very few studies that explore the internal tensions and deep disappointments within the merger movement.

4. H. Richard Niebuhr, *The Kingdom of God in America* (New York, 1937), 197.

5. For a remarkable artifact of ecumenical academia's sense of importance and faith in the power of their inherited tools, see Charles Harvey Arnold, *Near the Edge of Battle: A Short History of the Divinity School and the "Chicago School of Theology," 1866–1966* (Chicago, 1966).

6. For a cogent account of Cone's career, including the way his ideas changed over time, see Gary Dorrien, *Social Ethics in the Making: Interpreting an American Tradition* (London, 2012), 396–411. See also Lilian Calles Barger, *The World Come of Age: An Intellectual History of Liberation Theology* (New York, 2018). An accessible popular treatment, emphasizing Cone's insistence that the universality of the gospel was instantiated in its social particularization, is Brad East, "Jewish Jesus, Black Christ," *Christian Century*, January 22, 2022.

7. Keller's major works were *Apocalypse New and Then: A Feminist Guide to the End of the World* (Boston, 1996) and *Face of the Deep: A Theology of Becoming* (London, 2003).

8. For Murray's career, see Rosalind Rosenberg, *Jane Crow: The Life of Pauli Murray* (New York, 2017).

9. The German-centered tradition was perpetuated with distinction by Hans Frei, George Lindbeck, and Schubert Ogden, among others.

10. Gary Dorrien, "American Liberal Theology: Crisis, Irony, Decline, Renewal, Ambiguity," *Cross Currents* 55 (2006), 7, http://www.crosscurrents.org/dorrien200506 .htm.

11. Keller, *Face of the Deep*, 229.

12. Gary Dorrien, *The Making of American Liberal Theology: Crisis, Irony, and Postmodernity, 1950–2005* (Louisville, 2006), 512.

13. For Daly's career, see Sarah Lucia Hoagland and Marilyn Frye, eds., *Feminist Interpretations of Mary Daly* (University Park, PA, 2000).

14. Dorrien, "American Liberal Theology," 7.

15. Heather R. White, *Reforming Sodom: Protestants and the Rise of Gay Rights* (Chapel Hill, NC, 2015), esp. 6. This carefully documented study also demonstrates that ecumenical Protestants were often forceful and effective advocates for gay rights. White is one of few specialists in American religious history to argue that the progressive leaders of the ecumenical denominations "are perhaps the most influential of modern religious subjects" (8).

16. "Their women exchanged natural intercourse for unnatural, and in the same way also the men, giving up natural intercourse with women, were consumed with passion for one another. Men committed shameless acts with men and received in their own persons the due penalty for their error. . . . They know God's decree, that those who practice such things deserve to die." The meaning of this passage is highly contested. Some liberal theologians have accepted this passage as genuinely homophobic yet not problematic because it represents merely a feature of ancient Mediterranean culture that can be ignored today. Others have doubted Paul's generalized homophobia and interpreted the passage as directed at particular groups of contemporaries. Yet others find fault with many of the translations of this passage (rendered here in the New Revised Standard Version) from the original Greek. An ambitious review of the issues is Robert Jewett, *Romans: A Commentary* (Minneapolis, 2007). Leviticus 20:13, however, unambiguously mandates death for homosexual acts among males.

17. An account of this incident can be found in Stephen Bates, *A Church at War: Anglicans and Homosexuality* (London, 2004), esp. 37.

18. Thus utterance of Paul's is also a matter of dispute among biblical scholars, some of whom take it to be a later addition by some other author.

19. Judges 15:15 and 16:30.

20. Prominent among these were Global Ministries of the United Methodist Church, the World Mission of the United Presbyterian Church, and the Global Ministries Program jointly operated by the United Church of Christ and the Disciples of Christ.

21. Brian Stanley, *Christianity in the Twentieth Century: A World History* (Princeton, 2018), 366.

22. Philip Jenkins, *The Next Christendom: The Coming of Global Christianity*, 3rd ed. (New York, 2011), 270, 273, 275.

23. Melani McAlister, *The Kingdom of God Has No Boundaries: A Global History of American Evangelicalism* (New York, 2018).

24. I have addressed this dynamic at greater length in "The Global South, Christianity, and Secularization: Insider and Outsider Perspectives," *Modern Intellectual History* 17 (2020), 889–901.

25. For an effort to make the public more aware of Barber, see Charles M. Blow, "Modern-Day Moses," *New York Times*, March 9, 2022.

26. David Brooks, "The Good Faith," *New York Times*, February 6, 2022.

27. Raphael Warnock, quoted in "In a Georgia Runoff, Raising Uncomfortable Truths," *New York Times*, January 3, 2021, 12.

28. L. Harold DeWolf, *A Theology of the Living Church* (New York, 1953), 259, as quoted by Gary Dorrien, *The Making of American Liberal Theology: Crisis, Irony, and Postmodernity, 1950–2005* (Louisville, 2006), 21.

29. Harvey Cox, "Afterword," in Daniel Callahan, *The Secular City Debate* (New York, 1966), 188.

30. Van A. Harvey, *The Historian and the Believer: The Morality of Historical Knowledge and Christian Belief*, 3rd rev. ed. (Chicago, 1996), xxvi–xxvii.

31. Langdon Gilkey, "The Christian Congregation as a Religious Community," in James P. Wind and James W. Lewis, eds., *American Congregations: New Perspectives in the Study of Congregations* (Chicago, 1994), 107.

32. Spong's most important book was directly inspired by Robinson: John Shelby Spong, *Why Christianity Must Change or Die: A Bishop Speaks to Believers in Exile* (New York, 1999). Another exception to the avoidance of forceful argument was Marcus Borg, *Meeting Jesus Again for the First Time* (San Francisco, 1994). Borg co-authored several books with a liberal Catholic colleague, John Dominic Crossan, e.g., *The Last Week: What the Gospels Really Teach about Jesus' Final Days in Jerusalem* (San Francisco, 2006). Scottish scholar of the Hebrew Bible James Barr was also outspoken in several books that won attention in the United States, especially *Escaping from Fundamentalism* (London, 1984).

33. Tony Keddie, *Republican Jesus: How the Right Has Rewritten the Gospels* (Oakland, CA, 2020). Keddie does not write as an ecumenical Protestant and identifies himself religiously only as a former Catholic (8).

34. Sam Harris, *The End of Faith: Reason, Terror, and the Future of Reason* (New York, 2005), 20–21.

35. Philip Kitcher, *Life after Faith: The Case for Secular Humanism* (New Haven, CT, 2014), 24.

36. Marilynne Robinson, *Gilead* (New York, 2004); *Home* (New York, 2008); *Lila* (New York, 2014); *Jack* (New York, 2020); "Which Way to the City on a Hill?," *New York Review of Books*, July 18, 2019.

37. Despite this persistence of church affiliation on the part of African Americans, departures in the first two decades of the twenty-first century were noticeable enough to generate extensive media attention, e.g., Dara T. Mathis, "The Church's Black Exodus," *Atlantic*, October 11, 2020. Black intellectuals, moreover, have been among the most outspoken of American secularists, including W. E. B. Du Bois, James Baldwin, Harold Cruse, Ta-Nehisi Coates, and John McWhorter. For a history of this neglected tradition, see Christopher Cameron, *Black Freethinkers: A History of African American Secularism* (Evanston, IL, 2019).

38. Kristin Kobes Du Mez, *Jesus and John Wayne: How White Evangelicals Corrupted a Faith and Fractured a Nation* (New York, 2020), 6. See also Jesse Curtis, *The Myth of Colorblind Christians: Evangelicals and White Supremacy in the Civil Rights Era* (New York, 2021), 216–220.

39. Impressive documentation of how the United States was following the societies of Western Europe in a secularizing direction is in David Voas and Mark Chaves,

"Is the United States a Counterexample to the Secularization Thesis?," *American Journal of Sociology* 121 (2016), 1517–1566. See also my "Christianity and Its American Fate: Where History Interrogates Secularization Theory," in Joel Isaac, James T. Kloppenberg, Michael O'Brien, and Jennifer Ratner-Rosenhagen, eds., *The Worlds of American Intellectual History* (New York, 2017), 280–303.

40. David Hempton, "Organizing Concepts and 'Small Differences' in the Comparative Secularization of Western Europe and the United States," in David Hempton and Hugh McLeod, eds., *Secularization and Religious Innovation in the North Atlantic World* (New York, 2017), 352.

41. Brian Stanley, *Christianity in the Twentieth Century: A World History* (2018), 119.

42. Paul the Apostle described the followers of Jesus as "earthen vessels" (2 Corinthians 4:7, KJV); later translations refer to "clay pots."

Chapter 9. Beyond the Paradox of a Religious Politics in a Secular Society

1. Pew Research Center, "Faith on the Hill," February 4, 2021, https://www.pewforum.org/2021/01/04/faith-on-the-hill-2021/.

2. Of the more than 34 million men who registered for the draft during World War II, only about one-tenth of one percent were classified as conscientious objectors by the Selective Service Administration and then determined to be physically fit for military service. Of them, 25,000 accepted noncombatant duty in the military, 12,000 worked in camps operated by the Civilian Public Service, and 6,000 chose to go to prison rather than to cooperate in any way with the government. Anne M. Yoder, "Conscientious Objection in America: Primary Sources for Research" (Swarthmore College Peace Collection, February 2003), https://www.swarthmore.edu/library/peace/conscientiousobjection/co%20website/pages/HistoryNew.htm.

3. Winnifred Fallers Sullivan, *The Church State Corporation: Construing Religion in U.S. Law* (Chicago, 2020), traces the process by which the US Supreme Court broadened the conscientious objector exemption beyond historically recognized faiths and accepted any sincere belief as "religious." Sullivan argues the reluctance of the court to define what shall count as religion risks granting more and more sovereignty to anyone claiming to act religiously.

4. *Burwell v. Hobby Lobby Stores, Inc.,* 573 US 682 (2014).

5. *Fulton v. City of Philadelphia,* 141 S.Ct. 1868 (2021).

6. Linda Greenhouse, "Grievance Conservatives Are Here to Stay," *New York Review of Books,* July 1, 2021, 34.

7. The great power of this accusation—"you are hostile to religion!"—is revealed by the painstaking care with which the charge is refuted by Howard Gillman and

Erwin Chemerinsky, *The Religion Clauses: The Case for Separating Church and State* (New York, 2020), 161–176.

8. A well-argued history of secular-religious dialogue in the United States speculates that "liberal secularists" may soon be forced to conclude that "the language of religious freedom has become antithetical to secular governance" and must be replaced as a priority by "the language of equality." See David Sehat, *This Earthly Frame: The Making of American Secularism* (New Haven, CT, 2022), 265–266.

9. I have emphasized the significance of these two converging forces in *After Cloven Tongues of Fire: Protestant Liberalism in Modern American History* (Princeton, 2013), esp. 1–17.

10. John Dewey, *The Middle Works* (Carbondale, IL, 1982), 9:139.

11. Joe Bageant, *Deer Hunting with Jesus* (New York, 2007), 27, 33.

12. Claude S. Fischer and Michael Hout, *Century of Difference: How America Changed in the Last One Hundred Years* (New York, 2006).

13. For a sensitive reminder that many persons who seek some kind of transcendence do so without abusing their fellow human beings, see Tim Crane, *The Meaning of Belief: Religion from an Atheist's Point of View* (Cambridge, MA, 2017).

INDEX

A NOTE ON THE TYPE

This book has been composed in Arno, an Old-style serif typeface in the classic Venetian tradition, designed by Robert Slimbach at Adobe.